C000002258

FOCKE WULF FW190

IN COMBAT

FOCKE WULF FW190
IN COMBAT

ALFRED PRICE

First published in 1998
This edition first published in 2009

The History Press
The Mill, Brimscombe Port
Stroud, Gloucestershire, GL5 2QG
www.thehistorypress.co.uk

© Alfred Price, 1998, 2000, 2009

The right of Alfred Price to be identified as the Author
of this work has been asserted in accordance with the
Copyrights, Designs and Patents Act 1988.

All rights reserved. No part of this book may be reprinted
or reproduced or utilised in any form or by any electronic,
mechanical or other means, now known or hereafter invented,
including photocopying and recording, or in any information
storage or retrieval system, without the permission in writing
from the Publishers.

British Library Cataloguing in Publication Data.
A catalogue record for this book is available from the British Library.

ISBN 978 0 7524 5207 4

Typesetting and origination by The History Press
Printed in Great Britain

CONTENTS

Foreword   vii
Introduction   ix
Acknowledgements   xi

  1. Concept to Fruition   1
  2. Initial Flight Testing   10
  3. Focke Wulf Fw 190 in Service   25
  4. To Hijack a Focke Wulf   31
  5. Unsolicited Testimonials   38
  6. Units Equipped with Fw 190s, 27 July 1942   56
  7. In Action Against USAAF Heavy Bombers   59
  8. *Jabo* Pilot   75
  9. Units Equipped with Fw 190s, 17 May 1943   83
 10. *Jabos* Over Sicily and Italy   87
 11. Focke Wulf 190 Night-Fighters   96
 12. On the Eastern Front   102
 13. The Tables are Turned   105
 14. Units Equipped with Fw 190s, 31 May 1944   109
 15. No Place for a Beginner   113
 16. If Necessary, By Ramming   120
 17. The Luck of the Game   130
 18. Eastern Front *Jabo*   140
 19. Delivering the Focke Wulfs   148
 20. Enter the Long-Nosed Dora   156
 21. An Introduction to 'Beethoven'   161
 22. Night *Jabo*   169
 23. Units Equipped with Fw 190s, 9 April 1945   175
 24. Finale   181
 25. Fw 190s Post War   185

Appendices
 A. Production of Fw 190 and Ta 152   188
 B. Fw 190 Unit Prefixes   188
 C. Luftwaffe Flying Units   189
 D. Equivalent Wartime Ranks   190

Index   191

Focke Wulf Fw 190A-3s of one of the early production batches.

FOREWORD TO THE FIRST EDITION

BY GENERALLEUTNANT A.D. ADOLF GALLAND

When Alfred Price asked me to write this foreword, my first thought was, 'I suppose it will be yet another technical account of this aircraft, somebody listing the minute differences between the various sub-types'. How pleased I was to be proved wrong. The author is a flying man himself, and he has collected some fascinating stories about flying men, intended primarily for flying and ex-flying readers.

When I flew the Fw 190 for the first time, in 1942, I remember being greatly impressed by its high performance and its beautiful handling characteristics. So I was extremely interested to have my memories reawakened after all these years when reading the comprehensive report on this aircraft by the former enemy.

We in the Luftwaffe knew that the Fw 190 was good, but in 1941 and 1942 we had no way of knowing that it caused the enemy quite so much worry. Also of great interest to me was the British plan to mount an operation to hijack an Fw 190 from one of our airfields in France; the airfield at Abbeville was the home of *II. Gruppe* of

Jagdgeschwader 26, my former unit. Had the hijack operation been carried out it would have placed considerable risks on the men involved but it has to be admitted that the chances of success were high enough to justify such risks in wartime.

In this book the reader can sense the crushing pressure exerted on the Luftwaffe during the final year of the war. The outnumbered German fighter and fighter-bomber units, dwindling in strength and short of fuel, were hunted down in the air and on the ground. It provides a grim reminder of the penalties suffered when an enemy gains air supremacy over one's homeland, penalties which no German who experienced them will ever forget. Let us be sure that, whatever else we learn from the lessons of the past, the vital necessity of strength in air should never be far from our minds.

I wish Alfred Price success for his new book; his painstaking research and careful collation deserve it.

Adolf Galland

The author (right) pictured with the designer of the Focke Wulf Fw 190, Kurt Tank (centre), at Celle, Germany, in 1975 during the research for this book. On the left of Tank is Bernhard Jope, whose account of flying the unusual 'Beethoven' combination aircraft appears in this book.

INTRODUCTION

When the Focke Wulf Fw 190 first became operational, in the autumn of 1941, it gave its enemies a nasty shock. The new German fighter could out-run, out-climb and out-dive the Spitfire Mark V, the best machine the Royal Air Force then had available (see 'The Focke Wulf Fw 190 in Service').

So great was the apparent superiority of the new German fighter, that RAF personnel of all ranks ascribed to it an excellence even greater than it merited. If, in the spring of 1942, the C-in-C Fighter Command, Air Chief Marshal Sir Sholto Douglas, had been asked what he wanted most he would probably have answered, 'Several squadrons of Focke Wulf 190s!'

There was even a plan for a commando operation to seize an Fw 190 (see 'To Hijack a Focke Wulf') to discover its secrets. That plan was overtaken by events, however. In June 1942 a lost German pilot presented the RAF with an invaluable prize: an intact example of the Fw 190. Subsequent flight trials carried out in Britain (see 'Unsolicited Testimonials') revealed the Fw 190 for what it was – a well-designed high performance fighter with a few weaknesses but not many.

The Spitfire V was a fine example of the 'racehorse' type of fighter where its designer had concentrated on providing an aircraft with the best possible performance. The Fw 190 which eclipsed its combat abilities in several respects was, remarkably, built to a quite different formula. As designer Kurt Tank tells us (in 'Concept to Fruition'), his fighter was intended as a 'cavalry horse'. He designed a rugged fighter that could operate in primitive conditions, and take punishment as well as dish it out.

For about a year the Fw 190 enjoyed a clear margin of superiority over any opposing fighter type it was likely to meet in combat. Then, in the summer of 1942, the Spitfire Mark IX appeared. Fitted with a new and more powerful Merlin engine with two-stage supercharging, its performance was remarkably close to that of the German fighter.

From the beginning of 1943 German forces were pushed on to the defensive on each front in turn, as the Allies brought to bear their overwhelming superiority in manpower and resources (see 'In Action Against US Heavy Bombers'). Fighter and fighter-bomber units equipped with the Fw 190 now faced enemy air forces with aircraft comparable in quality, and superior in quantity.

The air war turned into a savage war of attrition which took a heavy toll of well-trained and experienced German pilots. Their replacements were far less capable. As the war progressed, the training received by German pilots deteriorated steadily, while that of their Allied counterparts improved. Superior numbers and better training gave the Allied fighter pilots a mighty advantage, which untutored resolution and personal self-sacrifice could not redress (see 'No Place for a Beginner'). During the final year of the war, the latest Allied fighters had the edge in performance over the Fw 190 (see 'The Tables are Turned').

During 1944 the Luftwaffe was forced into a life and death struggle to defend the German homeland against the powerful

American daylight bomber attacks. The heavily armed and armoured bombers were extremely difficult to knock down, however. The Luftwaffe tried many expedients, culminating in the creation of the so-called *Sturmgruppen*. These units were equipped with Fw 190s fitted with additional armour and powerful 30-mm heavy cannon. The volunteer pilots who flew them were to press home attacks to short range, and if they failed to destroy a bomber by conventional means they pledged to ram it (see 'If Necessary, By Ramming'). This harsh demand was soon allowed to lapse, however (see 'The Luck of the Game').

As a rugged high performance aircraft, the Fw 190 was an obvious choice for the role of fighter-bomber. The Fw 190 'Friedrich' and 'Gustav' were the main ground-attack versions. As the air war turned against Germany, these variants assumed growing importance. The slower types used earlier were quite unable to survive in the face of Allied air superiority. In 1944, despite the competing requirements for fighter variants, more than one third of all Fw 190s built were produced as ground-attack versions. Externally these were little different from the fighter sub-types, but internally there were significant differences. A shield of armour plate built into the underside and sides of the fuselage gave protection for the pilot, fuel tanks and engine from ground fire. At ground level, carrying a full ordnance load, these variants had a maximum speed of about 325 m.p.h. They were the fastest, and plane for plane the most effective armoured ground-attack aircraft to see action in the Second World War (see 'Jabo Pilot' and 'Eastern Front Jabo').

During the final months of the war the Luftwaffe came under crushing pressure on all fronts. Units were squeezed inexorably into the shrinking area under German control (see 'Delivering the Focke Wulfs', 'Enter the Long-Nosed Dora' and 'Night *Jabo*'). The Fw 190 also served as the upper half of the remarkable 'Beethoven' explosive aircraft, to be used in a devastating attack on Russian power stations. However, the Red Army overran the airfields earmarked for the operation before the attack could be launched (see 'An Introduction to "Beethoven"'). Fw 190s continued to fight hard until the final hours of the conflict (see 'Finale').

Alfred Price

ACKNOWLEDGEMENTS

In writing the first edition in 1975 and 1976 I was fortunate in receiving the generous assistance from many who knew the Fw 190 at first hand. First and foremost among these were the designer, Dipl. Ing. Professor Kurt Tank and Dipl. Ing. Hans Sander, who took it on its maiden flight. Then there are those who flew the aircraft in action: Adolf Dilg, Helmut Wenk, Werner Gail, Walther Hagenah, Fritz Buchholz, Ernst Schröder, Oskar Romm and Franz Züger. My good friend Bernhard Jope gave me the fascinating account of flying the 'Beethoven' composite aircraft. Unfortunately many of them are no longer with us, but their stories deserve to be told to future generations.

Many good friends provided photographs and information for this work. In particular I am grateful to Hans-Justus Maier, the historian of the present Fokker-VFW Company. Other contributors were Hans Redemann, Hanfried Schliephake, Derek Wood, Werner Girbig, Günther Heise, Robert Michulec, Franz Selinger, Jean-Bernard Frappe, Eddie Creek and J. Richard Smith. Cliff Minney did the line drawings.

I proffer particular thanks to my good friend and world-renowned artist Keith Ferris, for allowing me to use his superb painting of *Sturmgruppe* Fw 190s entitled, 'Real Trouble', on the dust jacket.

Finally, it is my hope that readers will get as much enjoyment from this book as I did, when I collected the material all those years ago.

CHAPTER 1

CONCEPT TO FRUITION

Of all the people associated with the Focke Wulf Fw 190, the name that springs most readily to mind is Professor Dr Ing. Kurt Tank, the firm's Technical Director. In 1975 the author was fortunate to be able to interview him, to discuss the genesis of the new fighter.

In the spring of 1938 the Air Ministry in Berlin requested design proposals for a new fighter type, to supplement the Messerschmitt Bf 109 that had recently entered service. The Focke Wulf Project Office submitted several alternatives, all based on the idea of a more rugged fighter than the Bf 109. The Air Ministry accepted one of the proposals and placed an order to construct prototypes. The new aircraft received the official designation Focke Wulf Fw 190. Kurt Tank outlined the reasoning behind his concept for the new fighter type.

'The Messerschmitt 109 and the British Spitfire, the two fastest fighters in the world at the time we began work on the Fw 190, could both be summed up as a very large engine on the front of the smallest possible airframe; in each case armament had been added almost as an afterthought. These designs, both of which admittedly proved successful, could be likened to racehorses: given the right amount of pampering and an easy course, they could outrun almost anything. But the moment the going became tough they were liable to falter.

'During World War I, I served in the cavalry and in the infantry. I had seen the harsh conditions under which military equipment had to work in wartime. I felt sure that a quite different breed of fighter would also have a place in any future conflict: one that could operate from ill-prepared front-line airfields; one that could be flown and maintained by men who had received only a short training; and one that could absorb a reasonable amount of battle damage and still get back. This was the background thinking behind the Focke Wulf 190; it was to be not a "racehorse" but a *Dienstpferd*, a cavalry horse.

'Obviously, if it was fitted with an engine developing the same power, a "racehorse" fighter with a lighter structure would always be able to outrun and outclimb the sort of fighter we had in mind; yet we could not allow this difference to become too great. The design problem centred round building a stronger airframe and one able to carry heavier weapons, without sacrificing too much in the way of flying performance.'

The layout of the Focke Wulf Fw 190 was entirely conventional – a low-winged monoplane with the nose-mounted engine driving a tractor airscrew. At the time this was considered the most efficient layout for a high performance fighter aircraft. The low wing gave least interference with the pilot's

The prototype Focke Wulf Fw 190, pictured in the experimental shop at Bremen during advanced assembly in the spring of 1939. Weber

vision, and also provided a convenient housing for the wide-track retractable undercarriage, allowing the undercarriage legs to be kept short.

'From my own flying experience I knew how important it was for a fighter pilot to have the best possible all-round view and we decided to fit a large frameless bubble canopy to the new fighter; later these became very fashionable, but in 1938 the idea was something of an innovation.

'We chose an air-cooled radial engine for the new fighter for two reasons. Firstly because such engines were far more rugged and could survive more punishment than the liquid-cooled types, and secondly

because the BMW Company was bench-running prototypes of a new engine, the 1,550 h.p. BMW 139, which developed somewhat more power than any liquid-cooled engine we had been offered. If our *Dienstpferd* was to come close in performance to other people's "race-horses" we would need all the engine power we could get.

'Some people have suggested that I had to fight a battle with the German Air Ministry to get them to accept the idea of a radial-engined fighter. That might make a good story but it is not history. In fact, there was quite a large body of official opinion in favour of such a fighter for the Luftwaffe. The Russian Rata fighter, several examples of which had been captured in Spain and brought back to Germany, had demonstrated the usefulness of a rugged fighter powered by an air-cooled engine. Looking further afield we saw that other nations, in particular the United States, were pushing ahead with the design and development of high-powered radial engines for fighters. We in Germany had no wish to lag behind in this field.'

Tank never had cause to regret the decision to fit an air-cooled radial engine to the Fw 190. In action the resilience of this type of power plant would be proved again and again. There were several occasions when these fighters had had a cylinder shot away and returned to make normal landings. In contrast, once its cooling system was hit and the liquid started to drain away, the subsequent running life of a liquid-cooled engine was measured in minutes.

Tank went to great pains to point out that although he was the head of the design team, the Fw 190 was the result of a team effort.

'I dare say a really good designer could have produced such a fighter all by himself. But it would have taken about eight years and at the end of that time nobody would have been in the least bit interested in it! A design for a fighting aircraft was of value only if it could be brought out quickly. So the closest collaboration between the members of the design team was essential. My assistant, Willi Käther, coordinated the work. Rudi Blaser with the help of the people in the drawing office designed the structure; he was a very clever practical engineer and usually seemed able to meet the strength requirement for a particular component for the lowest possible structural weight. Ludwig Mittelhüber headed the team at the Project Office responsible for the Fw 190. Hans Sander and Kurt Melhorn, the men who were to carry out the initial flying test programme, were brought in early. They had a great deal of say, especially about the layout of the cockpit, the positioning of the instruments and the design of the controls. Altogether, the team that prepared the design of the Fw 190 comprised about twelve men.'

By 1938 it was clear that the trend for the future development of military aircraft types would make them heavier and heavier. From the start, the Fw 190 was designed to accept this. The effect of this line of thinking is best exemplified by the undercarriage.

'For the design weight and estimated landing speed of the prototype aircraft, we calculated that an undercarriage to withstand a sinking speed of 2.5 m/sec [8.5 ft/sec] would be sufficient. But if the aircraft developed its maximum speed, weight and landing speed would all increase. That would result in considerably higher forces on the undercarriage during landing. So in the original stress calculations we allowed for a sinking speed not of 2.5 m/sec but of 4.5 m/sec [15 ft/sec]. And then we designed the undercarriage to be strong enough to take that. The move paid off. During its life the maximum loaded weight of the Fw 190 rose from 2.75 tons to more than twice that figure, but with few changes the undercarriage remained adequate. I have used the undercarriage as an example, but in fact several parts of the original structure were a great deal stronger than the minimum necessary.'

Although the new fighter had to be rugged it had also to handle well in the air.

Kurt Tank in the cockpit of an Fw 190. He often took part in the flight testing of his own designs. VFW-Fokker

The secret of this was to make the control surfaces large enough and to balance them with great care, both statistically and dynamically; if they were underbalanced they became too heavy and lost their effectiveness, if they were overbalanced this caused other problems. The design team did a lot of work to get a positive and immediate response from the flying controls. They decided to use rigid rods between the control column and the flying control surfaces instead of the more usual wires and pulleys. In service the latter were liable to stretch, and the resultant play made the controls less 'crisp'.

Once the prototype of the new fighter was airborne, late in the spring of 1939, the test pilots were able to explore its handling characteristics. Tank, too, joined in the testing of the new fighter.

'Hans Sander did the initial testing, then I flew the aircraft and found that she handled beautifully in the air. The work we had put into the flying controls had produced the results we wanted. I have always believed that a pilot should not have to use a great deal of muscle power to get an aeroplane to do what he wants. If the controls have been properly designed,

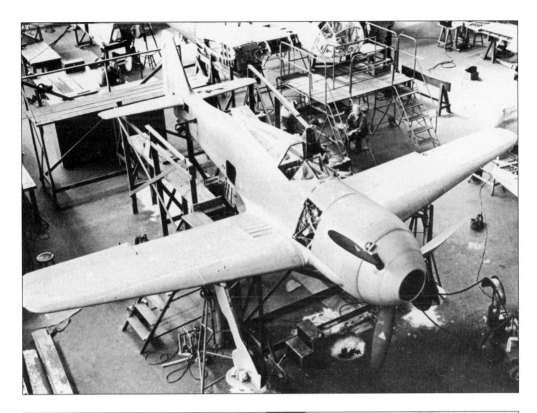

The first prototype nearing completion in the experimental shop. The ducted spinner was fitted only to this example of the Fw 190. via Redemann

he should be able to conduct most manoeuvres with only a finger and thumb on the stick. In combat a high rate of roll is essential for a fighter, so that the pilot can make rapid changes in his direction of flight. The aileron stick forces had, however, to be kept below a maximum of about eight pounds because a man's wrist cannot exert a force much greater than that. We succeeded in getting the stick forces down and finally I had the aileron controls as I wanted them. The aircraft followed the movement of the stick immediately and precisely, with no initial tendency to yaw. Compared with the ailerons, the other flying controls were relatively easy to design: the stick forces were not so critical for the elevators and the highest forces of all could be taken on the rudder pedals, because a man's legs are far stronger than his arms.'

Once the controls were correctly balanced, it was important to ensure that they stayed that way over a wide range of speeds. A fighter pilot did not want to have to re-trim the aircraft each time he moved to throttle. The team were so successful in this that they found that movable trim tabs were unnecessary. Small fixed trimming tabs were fitted to the ailerons, the elevators and the rudder. These were adjusted on the ground after the initial test flight, to compensate for the wide tolerances that occur with a mass-produced aircraft. The only system of trimming the aircraft in flight was in the elevator sense, and that was achieved using an all-moving tailplane.

The prototype Fw 190 flew well enough, although there was some trouble with the BMW 139 engine – the rear cylinders of the two-row radial were prone to overheating. To reduce the drag from the radial engine, the prototype was fitted with a special ducted

spinner. The cooling air was heated as it flowed past the cylinders and ejected from the rear of the spinner under pressure to provide a little extra thrust. During flight tests, however, it was found that the ducted spinner arrangement gave little reduction in drag. In truth the installation was not worth the bother, and early in the test programme the fighter was fitted with a normal cowling.

Even before the prototype Fw 190 began its flight trials, BMW was offering the new BMW 801 engine, then undergoing bench-testing. Quite apart from an extra 50 h.p., rising to 200 h.p. later, the new engine was more reliable and less prone to overheating than the BMW 139. Shortly after the first flight of the Fw 190, Focke Wulf received a contract to modify the fighter to take the BMW 801. The resultant aircraft, the Fw 190 V5, flew for the first time early in the spring of 1940.

'Although the extra 50 h.p. was useful, we found that the extra 160 kg [350 lb] of engine weight, plus the additional structure necessary to carry it, plus the weight of armour and the additional equipment the Luftwaffe now wanted, had increased all-up weight by about a quarter. The wing loading rose from the 1.6 kg/m² [38 lb/ft²] of the first prototype to 1.9 kg/m² [46 lb/ft²] and turning performance deteriorated accordingly. To restore the aircraft's previously pleasant handling characteristics we enlarged the wing by extending each tip by just over 50 cm [20 in] and reducing the amount of taper so that the outer sections were somewhat wider. In this way we increased the wing area by just over 3.25 m² [35 ft²] and lowered the wing loading to a more reasonable 1.5 kg/m² [35.8 lbs/ft²]. Later, to maintain the correct relationship between the wing and the tailplane, we

The first prototype, still unpainted, pictured during engine running and taxi trials conducted at the end of May 1939. via Redemann

made a proportional increase in the area of the latter. The wing and the tailplane of the low and medium altitude versions of the Fw 190 then remained unchanged throughout the remainder of the development life of the aircraft.'

There were problems with cooling the BMW 801 engine, though not as serious as with the BMW 139. And soon those difficulties were reduced to within acceptable limits. More serious were the troubles experienced with the engine control system, the *Kommandogerät*, fitted to the new engine.

'This was a rather clever device intended to save the pilot having to worry about the optimum relationship between altitude and fuel flow, fuel mixture, propeller pitch setting, ignition timing, engine revolutions and the selection of the correct supercharger gear. The pilot had simply to move one control, his throttle, and in theory the *Kommandogerät* did the rest. I say in theory, because at first the device did not work at all well. All sorts of things went wrong with it. One of the more disconcerting was the rather violent automatic switching-in of the high gear of the supercharger, as the aircraft climbed through 2,650 m [8,700 ft].

'Once I was carrying out a test with an early version of the Fw 190 which involved a loop at medium altitude. Just as I was nearing the top of the loop, on my back with little airspeed, I passed through 2,650 m and the high gear of the supercharger cut in with a jerk. The change in torque hurled the aircraft into a spin with such suddenness that I became completely disorientated. And, since there was a ground haze and an overcast and my artificial horizon had toppled, I had no

way of knowing which way was "up". Indeed, I never did find out whether it was an upright or an inverted spin. After considerable loss in altitude, I managed to recover from the spin. But the incident had given me a lot to think about. As soon as I landed, I was on the telephone to the BMW company. I told them that if they did not sort out their engine and its terrible *Kommandogerät*, I would do all in my power to see that somebody else's engine was fitted into the Fw 190! The *Kommandogerät* was made to work and it worked very well, but it took quite a battle on our part.'

When it went into action, in the summer of 1941, the Fw 190 demonstrated a clear margin of superiority over the Spitfire Mark V. With its powerful radial engine, the Focke Wulf *Dienstpferd* had the edge over the opposing 'racehorse'. This situation lasted for about a year, until the Spitfire Mark IX became operational, powered by the Merlin 61 engine fitted with a two-stage supercharger. This aircraft was superior to the Fw 190 at altitudes above 25,000 ft.

'We tried all sorts of things to improve the high altitude performance of the BMW 801, but really a completely new engine was needed. I had foreseen that something like this might happen. Early in 1941, before the Fw 190 entered service, I had spoken to Luftwaffe Generals Udet and Jeschonnek about it. I said they should put the Jumo 213 high altitude engine, then being bench-tested at Junkers, into series production so that we could have a high altitude version of the Fw 190 ready in case it was needed. General Hans Jeschonnek, then Chief of Staff of the Luftwaffe, had replied: "What is the point of that? We are not fighting any air battles at high altitude!" The result was that we lost about a year in the development of an effective high altitude engine, which we never really made up. In the end we did get the Fw 190D into service powered by the liquid-cooled Jumo 213, and it made a very good high altitude fighter. But it was not ready until late in the summer of 1944, by which time the battle for air superiority over Germany had been lost.'

The final development of the Fw 190 series of fighters to go into service was the Tank Ta 152, with the wingspan lengthened to 47 ft 6 in for high altitude operations. Power was from a liquid-cooled Jumo 213E engine with two-stage supercharging, which developed 1,730 h.p. at altitudes above 35,000 ft. This gave the fighter a maximum speed of 472 m.p.h. at 41,000 ft – very close to the limits of what is possible for an aircraft powered by a piston engine.

'On one occasion during the closing stages of the war I was flying a Ta 152. I had just taken off from Lagenhagen near Hanover, on my way to a conference at Cottbus. Suddenly the control tower called me and said there were, "Zwei Indiana über dem Gartenzaun" – two enemy fighters over the airfield. This placed me in a difficult position because, anxious to remain a

"civilian", I never flew with loaded guns. One could hardly expect the pilots of the two Mustangs to know that, however, and it is doubtful whether they would have acted any differently if they had known. As they came boring down after me I rammed open the throttle and switched in the water methanol injection. My aircraft surged forwards, accelerating rapidly. The Mustangs' closing speed swiftly fell to zero, then they diminished in size until they were mere specks in the distance. I have often wondered what those American pilots thought had happened to their "sitting duck".'

The Ta 152 became operational just before the war ended, but it never really had the chance to prove itself in action.

'There is little doubt that the *Dienstpferd* concept, upon which the Focke Wulf 190 was based, was sound. Soon after the war I was invited to the Society of British Aircraft Constructors' Display at Hatfield. I was walking into the Rolls-Royce chalet and amongst the people there was the RAF fighter ace "Johnny" Johnson. When we were introduced, he commented, "Oh, so you are the man responsible for the fighter which gave us all such a twitch in 1942 . . ."'

CHAPTER 2

INITIAL FLIGHT TESTING

Once the prototype had been built, it fell to the Focke Wulf test pilots to establish its performance envelope and discover any hidden vices or faults. Dipl. Ing. Hans Sander led the team responsible for the testing of the Fw 190.

Hans Sander first became interested in aeronautics in 1928, while studying mechanical engineering at the Technical High School at Aachen. He joined the academic flying group there and learned to fly. Later he designed a high performance glider and took part in its construction. In 1934, after gaining his degree as a Diploma Engineer, he entered the German Research Institute for Aeronautics in Berlin. There he trained as a *Flugbaumeister* (broadly the equivalent of the modern Project Engineer).

The three-year *Flugbaumeister* course was extremely thorough and included fifteen months at the flight test centre at Rechlin, working as an engineering test pilot. While there, Sander had the chance to try his hand flying almost every modern aircraft type at the centre. After completing the course successfully, in April 1937 he was offered a post as development test pilot at Focke Wulf. In the years that followed he took part in the testing of the company's new aircraft: the Fw 187 ground-attack aircraft, the Fw 189 reconnaissance aircraft and the four-engined Fw 200 transport.

'By the time the Focke Wulf 190 was taking shape, I was head of the firm's prototype flight test department. From the very beginning, I was involved with new fighters. I was there when we designed and built the wooden mock-up to see that everything would fit in. I had a lot to do with the cockpit layout. Then the first pieces of metal were cut and as she gradually took shape, I came to know her intimately. By the middle of May 1939 the new fighter was complete and we carried out the engine-running trials. Then I conducted the taxiing trials. Those proved little, because the small airfield at Bremen did not allow much of a ground run if one was to stop before hitting the fence at the other end. By this stage, however, I knew the aircraft so well that I was confident that she would fly safely when the time came.'

On 1 June 1939 everything was ready, and the prototype was wheeled out for her maiden flight. Sander started the engine and taxied out to the end of the runway. Then, after a final detailed check that everything was as it should be, he pushed open the throttle.

'With 1,550 h.p. pulling it the aircraft surged forwards, accelerating rapidly to flying speed. At a speed of just over 160 km/h [100 m.p.h.], she lifted off the ground and climbed away. At that time a retractable undercarriage was

The first prototype Fw 190, pictured at about the time of its maiden flight from Bremen on 1 June 1939. During its initial flight trials, the aircraft carried the civil registration D-OPZE. via Redemann

still a novelty. People still did not trust them to work properly, and it was usual for an aircraft making its first flight to do so with the undercarriage locked down. During the first flight of the Fw 190, I had to weigh the chances of undercarriage failure against those of an engine failure at low altitude. If I was unable to glide back to the airfield, I would have to make an emergency landing in one of the neighbouring fields. And if the surface was not flat, a wheels-down landing might result in the aircraft nosing over and ending up on its back. So, immediately after take-off, I retracted the undercarriage of the Fw 190.

'Once airborne, I spiralled up to about 1,800 m [6,000 ft], keeping over the airfield so those on the ground could see what was happening. I made a couple of high speed runs to see how she handled close to her maximum speed. Then I made turns at different speeds, and noted the stick forces that were necessary. Aerodynamically, she handled beautifully. The controls were light, positive and well-balanced. Throughout the initial flight I never had to make use of the tailplane trim. I suppose most test pilots would have made at least a roll in the new aircraft, but I did no aerobatics during the maiden flight of the Fw 190. I was quite happy to leave such fancy flying until later in the

Hans Sander flew the Fw 190 during its maiden flight and played a major part in testing the many variants during the years that followed. Sander

With Hans Sander at the controls, the first prototype Fw 190 is seen during its flight trials. By this time the original ducted spinner had been removed and replaced with a conventional radial cowling. VFW-Fokker

test programme, when I knew more about her. At this stage my task was merely to "taste" the handling characteristics of the new fighter.'

For the maiden flight Sander wore a thin flying suit over his normal underwear, socks, ordinary shoes and a flying helmet with the oxygen mask hanging loose. Yet soon after take-off he began to sweat profusely. The rear of the engine was hard up against the front wall of the cockpit, and his feet on the rudder pedals were either side of the engine accessories.

'The temperature in the cockpit rose to 55°C, I felt as though I was sitting with my feet in a fire! The heat was bearable, but very uncomfortable. Potentially more dangerous was the fact that the sealing round the cockpit was poor in places, and the exhaust fumes began to seep in. Fortunately I always flew with my oxygen mask (since a near-disaster at Rechlin, when I suffered a dose of carbon monoxide poisoning whose effects lasted for about six months). I clamped my mask to my face and made almost the whole of the maiden flight breathing pure oxygen.'

A further problem concerned the undercarriage retraction mechanism, where the up-lock failed to engage properly.

'If I pulled any "G", the undercarriage legs were liable to sag down. In the cockpit the red "undercarriage unlocked" light came on. The prototype Fw 190 was fitted with a hydraulic retraction system (on production aircraft it was electrical). During its operation the hydraulic system ran at an overload pressure of about 120 bars [1,700 lbs/in^2]. I knew that if I operated it at overload pressure too often to get the undercarriage to lock up again,

the hydraulic pump was liable to break down. So the system had to be treated with care. This was a minor problem, however, nothing more.'

After about twenty minutes at medium altitude, the time came to try the first landing. To leave as little as possible to chance, before descending Sander carried out a couple of stalls and a simulated landing. He needed to ensure that the fighter's low speed handling characteristics held no unpleasant surprises. Everything seemed in order so he throttled back and went down, extended the flaps and undercarriage and made a perfectly normal landing. There was no drama of any sort – the last thing a test pilot wants with a new aircraft.

After the flight, Sander had the aircraft put on jacks to discover what was wrong with the undercarriage up-lock.

'I saw the cause of the trouble: the locking catch was not engaging the lug on the undercarriage leg properly. So I filed away some metal from the inside of the catch. That reduced but did not eliminate the incidence of unlocking during subsequent test flights. We also tightened up the up-lock mechanism.'

Following each subsequent failure of the up-lock to engage properly, the mechanism was further tightened: this nearly caused an embarrassing situation for Sander. On 3 July he took the new fighter to Rechlin, in preparation for a demonstration flight before Hermann Göring, General Udet and other senior Luftwaffe officers. As he approached to land Sander released the up-lock before extending the undercarriage – and found it would not budge! Fortunately he knew the system well enough to 'trick' it, and he lowered the wheels for a normal landing.

Test of the ejector seat for the Fw 190, designed by Hans Sander. Lowering the correctly weighted dummy pilot into the cockpit.

The dummy and seat in position.

Test firing of the seat.

Seat comes to rest on the wooden structure protecting the tail. The aircraft used in the trial was the twenty-second Fw 190A-0 pre-production aircraft. VFW-Fokker

Early in 1940 the new and more powerful BMW 801 engine became available and this was fitted into the Fw 190 V5 in place of the smaller BMW 139. It is believed that this photograph depicts the actual fitting of the BMW 801 into the V5, in the experimental shop at Bremen. Note the fan mounted on the front of the engine, to assist in cooling the cylinders.

The V5 depicted at about the time of its first flight, in April 1940. This aircraft still carries the smaller, more tapered wing as on the prototype. VFW-Fokker

Once on the ground at Rechlin, Sander had the aircraft jacked up and he slackened off the up-lock mechanism. The subsequent demonstration flight went off without a hitch, but obviously simple readjustments could not be relied upon to solve that particular problem.

'The reason for the poor performance of the up-lock mechanism was that it was not strong enough for the job it had to do. The catch was cut out of a piece of sheet metal, and was operated by a simple wire cable. I became convinced that such a mechanism would never be suitable for mass production. After a lot of discussion we removed the locking catch, and substituted it with a bomb release shackle. That proved more than strong enough for the job and we had no further trouble from that quarter.'

Another difficulty that manifested itself during the test programme concerned the canopy opening system. It was quite impossible to open the hood at speeds greater than 270 m.p.h.

'This meant I could not abandon the aircraft if there was an emergency at high speed – not a prospect to cheer a pilot flying an unproven aircraft. No matter how hard one tried to wind open the hood with the mechanism provided, the aerodynamic forces held it firmly closed. Rudi Blaser worked out a system using bungee rubber to assist in opening the hood, but that did not work either. When operated at high speed, the hood would open a little then slam shut. Next he tried a more powerful system using compressed air, but that was little better.

'Obviously we needed to know more about the aerodynamic forces round the canopy, so we fitted sensors to take pressure measurements at high speed. From these we calculated that about 50 h.p. was necessary to overcome the forces holding the canopy shut. We needed power of a somewhat higher order than previously used to wrench it open. Finally Blaser designed a new system using a 20-mm cartridge firing against a piston, to push the canopy rearwards and force it to jettison cleanly. The first time we tried out the system on the ground we did not lose the canopy, we lost the piston! The force of the explosion tore the piston away from the hood and it emerged from the fuselage at high speed. Fortunately, nobody was in the way! Fitted with stronger attachment points, the explosive hood jettison mechanism worked very well. We were apprehensive that the hood might be blown straight and smash into the fin, but so far as I know this never happened. Once the hood was back far enough to break the aerodynamic lock, the airflow got underneath it and lifted it clear.'

Once the canopy jettison problem was solved, Sander became interested in the idea of using an explosive charge to eject the pilot from the Fw 190. Kurt Tank said he could not afford to divert his main design team to work on this, so Sander designed a simple ejector seat and had it built. The seat was powered by an explosive cartridge, but the latter was not powerful enough to lift a man clear of the tail if the aircraft was moving at high speed. Ground firing trials with a weighted dummy revealed that the project required more effort than Sander could give it, in addition to his other duties. So the idea was shelved. 'After the war I heard that Sir James Martin in Britain had perfected the design of a similar explosive ejector seat. But when I learned that it had taken several years

A wooden model undergoing wind-tunnel tests early in 1940, to determine the airflow characteristics of the enlarged wing before it was fitted to the V5 prototype. VFW-Fokker

A line-up of prototype and pre-production Fw 190s at Bremen in the spring or early summer of 1940. The second and third aircraft from the left are the first prototype and V5 respectively. The other aircraft in the line-up are of the A-0 pre-production version. All the aircraft have the early type tapered wing, fitted to the initial prototypes and the first eight pre-production aircraft. VFW-Fokker

These photographs are believed to depict the Fw 190 V7, the first aircraft of this type to be fitted with armament; it carried two 7.9-mm MG17 machine-guns above the engine and two more in the wing root, with all four weapons synchronized to fire through the airscrew. In these photographs the aircraft is seen levelled off ready for firing at the stop butts, with boxes in position to collect the links and the cartridge cases as they fall clear. VFW-Fokker

Aircraft from the first production batch of Fw 190A-1s, pictured at Marienburg, probably in July 1941. Included in this line-up are the 8th, 12th and 14th aircraft of this series. VFW-Fokker

of full-time work to get it to function properly, I did not feel too badly about my "failure".'

Like most test pilots, Hans Sander made it a point of honour to make every effort to land his aircraft safely following a failure in flight. A pile of smoking wreckage in a field was not only an expensive waste, but its cause might not be immediately obvious and it could set back the entire test programme.

'To minimize the risks, I arranged my test flights so that if there was an engine failure I could usually glide back to the airfield. During the early part of the flight test programme, engine failures were not all that uncommon. On more than one

occasion this forethought stood me in good stead.

'I never abandoned a Focke Wulf 190 in the air, though I must admit there were occasions when I came close to doing so. Once I was airborne in one of the early prototypes when suddenly there was a flash and the cockpit began to fill with dense and acrid smoke. I clamped on my mask and selected pure oxygen, then reduced speed and wound back the canopy.

'I was able to see well enough to realize that the smoke was coming up from below my feet. Fire is the greatest hazard of all in an aircraft: if it reached the fuel tank under my seat, my chance of survival would be slim. Many pilots, I know, would have got out there and then. But I decided to carry on. As an engineer I was curious to know the cause of the trouble. It seemed like an electrical fire. If it was, and if it had not yet taken hold, the way to stop it was to remove the source of current. But the only way to stop the generator, with the electrical system as it then was, was to stop the engine. I feathered the propeller, shut the fuel cock and switched off the ignition. The engine came to a stop and, to my intense relief, the smoke died away. The Fw 190 was now a glider, but I had done a lot of flying in gliders so that posed no great problem. As usual I had conducted the trial with sufficient altitude to glide back to the airfield in the event of an engine failure, and this was one occasion when the precaution paid off. My landing took everyone at the airfield by surprise: nobody heard me coming and the first thing they knew was when I was down. The landing was perfectly normal and the aircraft suffered no further damage. Subsequent examination revealed that the insulation had rubbed off some of the electrical wiring, and the engine vibration caused an intermittent short circuit of the main 3 kW electrical system. No wonder there had been a lot of smoke! After the incident the electrical system was altered so that the generator could be switched out of circuit without shutting down the engine.'

The Fw 190 powered by the BMW 801 engine, the V5, first flew in April 1940. The 18-cylinder BMW 801 was about 350 lb heavier than the BMW 139, so a stronger mounting was necessary to support it. To compensate for the increased weight in the nose, the fuselage had to be redesigned. To keep the centre of gravity in the right place,

the cockpit was moved further back. That led to a slight deterioration in the pilot's field of vision forwards and downward. However, this did confer a great bonus:

'Since the engine and the cockpit were now further apart, at last one could fly in the new fighter without having one's feet gently roasted! With all the extra weight, the wing loading shot up and the new version did not handle so well as the earlier prototypes. To overcome this problem, it was fitted with a redesigned wing of greater area.'

In August 1940 Sander was flying in the V5 when he was involved in what could have been a very nasty accident. He had not been airborne long when the gun access panel immediately in front of the cockpit started to come adrift. The panel was hinged at the rear. If the front fasteners gave way, the airflow would get underneath the panel and slam it back over the cockpit.

'I throttled back and cut short the test, landing back at Bremen without first making my usual circuit of the airfield. I set down the aircraft normally and the panel remained in place. But as I was rolling to a halt there was an enormous crash and the next thing I knew I was upside down with the aircraft on top of me. Expecting the fighter to burst into flames at any moment, I fought to get out and finally did so with some cuts and bruises. What had happened was that the ground staff had been using a quiet period to lay out some camouflage netting and I had collided with the trailer carrying it. The tractor driver had strict instructions not to drive on to the airfield. But he had not expected me back so early and was keen to get the work completed before my

By the summer of 1941, Fw 190 production was getting into its stride. Between the beginning of July and the end of the year the Marienburg plant delivered a total of 133 of these aircraft to the Luftwaffe. The Arado plant at Warnemünde began production in August and produced a further fifty-two, while the Ago plant at Oschersleben began in October and added thirty-five more.

(*Above*) A general view of one of the production lines for early series Fw 190s.

Lowering the BMW 801 engine into place on an early production aircraft. VFW-Fokker

Testing the undercarriage retraction system. The Fw 190 was unusual among Second World War fighters in that it employed an electrical retraction system. VFW-Fokker

The final tuning of the engine. VFW-Fokker

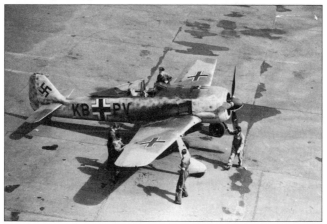

A pre-flight walk round by the production test pilot, prior to take-off. VFW-Fokker

arrival. Fortunately I had not been going fast at the moment of impact and the aircraft was not seriously damaged.'

Hans Sander's task as test pilot was to explore the safe operating limits of the Fw 190. Also, with the help of the design team, he worked to bring the new fighter to the point where it would be accepted by the service authorities. When service pilots at the Rechlin test centre tried out the aircraft, they too became enthusiastic about the Fw 190's high performance and excellent handling characteristics. The Fw 190 was ordered into large-scale production.

'Looking back, I believe that the fact that I was a qualified engineer as well as a test pilot did much to ease the passage of the Fw 190 into service and, later, through its development life. I think Kurt Tank agreed with this, because later he commented that he would not employ a test pilot who was not a qualified engineer. During the development phase it greatly speeded

events when I was able to suggest workable engineering solutions to problems I had encountered in the air.

'Reading about aircraft which have proved successful, one often hears how the test pilot got out after the maiden flight and proclaimed that here was a world-beating flying machine. Such statements might make nice copy for the firm's publicity people, but in my experience the reality of initial test flying is less theatrical. For the record, I never said any such thing after the maiden flight of the Focke Wulf 190. I am an engineer and during my training I had been taught to be cautious. After the first flight I told the members of the design team what I had learned about the new fighter – which was not a great deal, since the flight had lasted only half an hour. I said that so far as I tried them the controls were light, positive and well-balanced, the trim was excellent and the aircraft had not demonstrated any vices; but about the heat coming into the cockpit and that undercarriage up-lock . . . .'

CHAPTER 3

FOCKE WULF FW 190 IN SERVICE

In the summer of 1941 the first batch of Fw 190A-1s, the initial production version of the new fighter, began leaving the factory at Marienburg. By the end of July, twenty-two of the new fighters had been delivered to the Luftwaffe. The 6th *Staffel* of *Jagdgeschwader 26*, commanded by Oberleutnant Walter Schneider and based at Moorseele in Belgium, became the first operational unit to receive the new type.

Some sources have said that the new German fighter's existence was unknown to the Royal Air Force at this time. This is not true. The Air Ministry *Weekly Intelligence Summary* dated 13 August 1941, a secret document issued to all RAF units and made available to aircrew, carried the following report:

FW 190 FIGHTER

A certain number of these new fighters have been produced, but information available is very scanty. The general design is said to be based on American practice and the aircraft is probably a low-wing monoplane with a fairly short fuselage and a span of about thirty feet. This new aircraft is fitted with a two-bank radial, an engine of the same type as that in the Dornier 217. It is definitely known that this particular machine had to be fitted with an auxiliary mechanically-driven fan to keep the engine temperatures within reasonable limits. It is also reported that it

is equipped with a very large airscrew and that the undercarriage is extraordinarily high in order to give the necessary ground clearance. Rough estimates show that the speed of the Fw 190 is somewhere between 370 and 380 mph at 18–20,000 ft.

The brief report was accurate, except in two respects. Firstly, the propeller fitted to the Fw 190 was not particularly large. Secondly, and more importantly, the report underestimated the maximum speed of the Fw 190 by about 30 m.p.h.

By September the whole of *II./JG 26*, established at thirty aircraft, had been re-equipped with Fw 190s. Soon afterwards the RAF pilots reported contacts with the new German fighter. Following the action on 18 September a combat report noted the destruction of '. . . a Curtiss Hawk (or Fw 190) . . .' Almost certainly this referred to the Focke Wulf flown by the commander of *II./JG 26*, Hauptmann Walter Adolph, who was shot down and killed that day.

Three days later, escorting Blenheims attacking the power station at Gusnay near Bethune, the Polish No. 315 Squadron reported that its Spitfires had destroyed '. . . one unknown enemy aircraft with a radial engine . . .' Almost certainly it was the Fw 190 flown by Leutnant Ulrich Dzialas of *8./JG 26*, who was killed.

In service the Fw 190 suffered initially from a resurgence of the old overheating

An Fw 190A-1 of the 6th *Staffel* of *Jagdgeschwader 26* which, based at Moorseele in Belgium, was the first operational unit to receive this type; deliveries began in July 1941.

Cases of the engine overheating were frequent when the Fw 190 first went into service. Sometimes this led to fires, as in the case of this foam smothered A-1 belonging to *II./JG 26*.

Ground crewmen removing the airscrew from an Fw 190. The VDM constant speed three-blade propeller had a blade diameter of 10 ft 10 in (3.3 m). VFW-Fokker

troubles with the BMW 801 engine. There were even cases of these engines catching fire. After the loss of some aircraft to this cause, pilots were forbidden to fly over the sea beyond gliding range from the coast until the problem was cured.

In spite of the slowly mounting evidence, a few more months would elapse before the RAF Intelligence Service committed itself to giving a positive identification to the new fighter. In the issue dated 29 October 1941, the *Weekly Intelligence Summary* carried the following report: 'In recent weeks a radial-engined type of fighter has been encountered by the RAF and has been reported as a French aircraft, the Bloch 151, and as a new type of German fighter, the Fw 190. There is as yet insufficient evidence to say with certainty what the new aircraft is.'

Meanwhile, production of the Fw 190A-1, then the A-2, proceeded apace. By the end of 1941 more than 200 of these fighters had been delivered to the Luftwaffe.

By the beginning of 1942 RAF Intelligence had at last established beyond doubt that the new German fighter was indeed the Focke Wulf 190. Also, from the reports of disgruntled fighter pilots who had encountered it in combat, it became clear that radial-engined aircraft were formidable opponents. The Focke Wulf had a clear margin in performance over the Spitfire V, the best aircraft RAF Fighter Command then had available.

During the spring of 1942 all six *Gruppen* of *Jagdgeschwader* 2 and 26 had re-equipped with the Fw 190. Between them these units mustered about 260 of these formidable fighters. By then the earlier engine troubles had been cured, allowing the pilots to exploit to the full the capabilities of the Fw 190.

For RAF Fighter Command this was the most difficult period since the end of the Battle of Britain. For example, during Circus Operation No. 178 on 1 June, eight bomb-carrying Hurricanes attacked a target in northern Belgium. Seven squadrons of Spitfire Vs from the Hornchurch and Biggin Hill Wings provided close escort and four squadrons from the Debden Wing provided target support. Positioned by radar, the fighter ace Hauptmann 'Pips' Priller led some forty Fw 190s of Ist and IIIrd *Gruppen* of *Jagdgeschwader* 26 to 'bounce' the raiding force from out of the sun. The Debden Wing took the force of the attack and suffered the loss of eight Spitfires, including that flown by its commander. Five more Spitfires returned with battle damage. No Focke Wulf suffered serious damage during the encounter.

The following day was another bad one for the RAF. Two wings of Spitfires flew a 'Rodeo' operation, a large scale fighter sweep, through the St Omer area. The Luftwaffe usually ignored such incursions, but not this time. Focke Wulfs of Ist and IInd *Gruppen* of JG 26 delivered a massed attack concentrating on No. 403 (Canadian) Squadron led by the redoubtable Squadron Leader Alan Deere. There followed a desperate seven-minute brawl, in which seven Spitfires were shot down and two suffered serious damage. Again, no Focke Wulf suffered serious damage.

The RAF's long-term answer to the Fw 190 was the Mark IX version of the Spitfire, fitted with an improved engine with two-stage supercharging. But the introduction of this aircraft would take time, and until then Fighter Command would have to do the best it could with inferior equipment. How useful it would be if an example of the Fw 190 could be captured so that its weaknesses might be learned and, perhaps, exploited . . . .

The second *Gruppe* to re-equip with the Fw 190 was *III./JG 26*, which received its first aircraft in September 1941. In the foreground is the unit's commander, Major Gerhard Schöpfel. In December 1941 Oberstleutnant Adolf Galland relinquished command of *JG 26* to become Inspector of Fighters. Gerhard Schöpfel then assumed command of the entire *Geschwader*. Schöpfel

Hauptmann Heino Greisert, the commander of *II./JG 2*, pictured during his birthday celebrations at Beaumont Le Roger, France, in 1942. via Pegg

FOCKE WULF FW 190A-3

Type: Single-seat general-purpose day-fighter.

Armament: Two Mauser MG 151 20-mm cannon with 200 r.p.g., one mounted in each wing root and synchronized to fire through the airscrew. Two Rheinmetall MG 17 7.9-mm machine-guns with 1,000 r.p.g., mounted on top of the engine cowling and synchronized to fire through the airscrew. Two Oerlikon MG/FF 20-mm cannon with 55 r.p.g., mounted in the wings and firing outside the propeller disk.

Power Plant: BMW 801D-2 air-cooled 14-cylinder radial engine rated at 1,700 h.p. for take-off, driving a VDM three-bladed constant speed airscrew. Fuel capacity: 115 Imp. gal. (525 l) in two self-sealing tanks under the cockpit. Provision for one 66 Imp. gal. (300 l) drop-tank on the fuselage rack.

Weights: (empty, equipped) 7,110 lb (3,225 kg); (operational, take-off) 8,770 lb (3,977 kg).

Dimensions: Span: 34 ft 5½ in (10.51 m); length, 28 ft 10½ in (8.8 m); wing area 197 sq ft (18.3 m²).

Performance: Maximum speed, 418 m.p.h. (673 k.m./h.) at 21,000 ft (6,400 m); initial rate of climb, 2,830 ft/min (14.58 m/sec); time to 26,240 ft (8,000 m), 12 min.; service ceiling 34,770 ft (10,600 m).

CHAPTER 4

TO HIJACK A FOCKE WULF

'The art of war is divided between force and stratagem. What cannot be done by force must be done by stratagem.'

Frederick the Great

Obviously it would be of inestimable value to RAF Fighter Command if an airworthy example of the Fw 190 could be captured and its secrets probed. Yet that was a requirement far easier to state than to achieve. Captain Philip Pinckney, a Commando officer, learned of the requirement from his good friend, test pilot Jeffrey Quill. Undeterred by the many obvious difficulties, Pinckney devised a plan to gain that end. For brass-necked effrontery it can have few equals in military history, and it might just have succeeded. His proposal is reproduced in full below.

MOST SECRET AND URGENT
To: Officer Commanding No. 12 Commando
From: Captain Pinckney, E Troop, No. 12 Commando

Sir,
I understand that as a matter of great urgency and importance a specimen Focke Wulf 190 is required in this country. I attach a proposal for procuring one of these aircraft.

I have the honour to request that this, my application to be allowed to undertake the operation described, may be forwarded as rapidly as possible through the correct channels to the Chief of Combined Operations. I further propose that the pilot to accompany me should be Mr Jeffrey Quill who is a close friend of mine, and as a well known test pilot of fighter aircraft is well qualified to bring back the plane. He is also young, active, a yachtsman, and a man in every way suitable to carry out the preliminary approach by land and sea.

If Mr Quill cannot be allowed to undertake this operation, perhaps a substitute could be made available from the Free French Forces. I am most anxious to be allowed to volunteer for this operation.
I have the honour to be,
Sir,
Your obedient servant
(signed) P.H. Pinckney

23.6.42

A Fw 190 warming up its engine at a dispersal point with the unarmed ground crewmen standing nearby: an ideal target for the hijack attempt.

1. Object: to bring back to this country undamaged a Focke Wulf 190.
2. Forces Required:
   One MGB [motor gunboat] equipped with DF [direction-finding radio] apparatus, to carry a folbot [collapsible canoe] to within two miles of the coast of France.
   One folbot equipped with wireless transmitter.
   One officer of a Commando.
   One specially selected pilot.

Method
3. (Day 1)
   a. On the night of D1 the MGB, carrying the officers and folbot, will leave England after dark and proceed at best speed to within one or two miles of the French coast off a selected beach.
   b. On reaching the beach the folbot will be carried inland and hidden in a wood or buried in the dunes. The officers will lie up during the following day.
4. (Day 2)
   a. After laying up all day the officers will move inland at nightfall until they are within observation range of a fighter aerodrome.

5. (Day 3)
   a. On D3 the officers will keep the aerodrome under observation and plan the attack for the start of nautical twilight [i.e., just before sunrise] on D4.
   b. During the night of D3 the officers will penetrate the aerodrome defences by stealth and will conceal themselves as near as possible to a selected Focke Wulf aircraft.
6. (Day 4)
   a. At the start of nautical twilight on D4, when the aircraft are warmed up by the ground mechanics, the two officers will take the first opportunity to shoot the ground mechanics of the selected plane as soon as it has been started up. The pilot officer will take off in the machine and return to England. The commando officer will first ensure the safe departure of the aircraft, and will then withdraw to a previously reconnoitred hideup. Should no opportunity to seize the aircraft have presented itself, the officers will withdraw to a hideup and make another attempt next morning.
   b. During the night of D4 the conmando officer will return to the concealed folbot.
7. (Day 5)
   a. After nautical twilight on D5 or during the succeeding night, this officer will launch the folbot and be picked up by an MGB.
   b. The MGB should be off the coast for two hours before nautical twilight on D5, D6 or D7 providing the weather is calm. If the weather is unsuitable, the MGB should come on the first suitable morning. The officer, after launching the folbot, will paddle to a pre-arranged bearing. The MGB, making due allowance for the day and consequent set of the tide, will proceed on a course to intercept the folbot. In addition the officer will make wireless signals, which will be picked up by the MGB using DF gear.

Notes

8. Selected aerodrome
   a. The selection of an aerodrome will be dependent on intelligence not at present available to me. The requirements are:
      1. Within 20 miles of landing beach which is not too strongly defended, and which has a hinterland of dunes or woods offering a hiding place for the folbot.
      2. Within observation range or a few miles of a covered approach or a wood or place of concealment.
   b. It is thought that possibly Abbeville aerodrome might be suitable with a landing made on the Somme estuary. The Cherbourg Peninsula, entailing a cliff-climbing on landing, might give a good chance of making an undiscovered landing, providing a suitable aerodrome is nearby.
9. Return of the plane.
   Arrangements must be made with Fighter Command to ensure that the pilot officer is not shot down by our fighters on returning with the captured aircraft. It is suggested that these arrangements should not be dependent upon wireless or on the officers taking distinctive markings or signalling apparatus with them. Possibly Fighter Command could be instructed not to shoot down any enemy Focke Wulf 190 appearing over the coast during specified times on selected days. In addition the undercarriage could be lowered for identification. If a Focke Wulf 190 after all is unprocurable on the aerodrome, a Messerschmitt 109F could be brought back instead. I understand that its acquisition would also be valuable.

The cockpit of the Fw 190A-3.

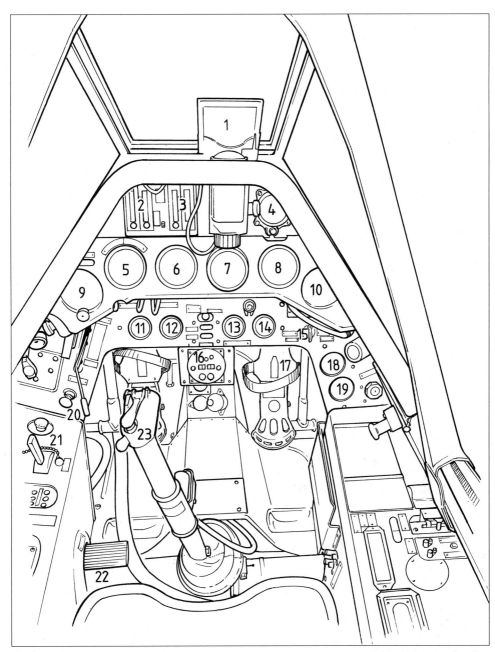

A plan of the cockpit of the Fw 190A-3.

Key: 1. Revi 16B reflector sight.

2. Armament switches and round counters.

3. Armament switches and round counters.

4. FuG 16 ZY radio homing indicator.

5. Airspeed indicator.

6. Artificial horizon.

7. Rate of climb/descent indicator.

8. Repeater compass.

9. Altimeter.

10. Engine r.p.m. gauge.

11. Fuel and oil pressure gauge.

12. Oil temperature gauge.

13. Fuel contents gauge.

14. Airscrew pitch indicator.

15. Fuel gauge selector switch.

16. Bomb release control panel.

17. Rudder pedal.

18. Oxygen flow indicator.

19. Oxygen pressure gauge.

20. Landing gear up-lock release.

21. Tailplane trim switch.

22. Throttle.

23. Control column, with gun firing button.

10. Date.
   The landing should be made on a rising tide to cover footprints and also on a dark night to achieve surprise.
11. Alternative return of Commando officer. If it is considered an unacceptable naval risk to bring back an MGB to pick up the Commando officer, this officer could either paddle on a course pre-arranged by Fighter Command and eventually be picked up by an RAF rescue launch or, as a third alternative method of withdrawal, he could be instructed to make his way back through occupied France.
12. Other considerations.
   a. Food. The officers will be equipped with ten days' compressed rations.
   b. Preparation. The officers should have ample time to train together for a period which need not exceed ten days. Training should also be carried out on the MGB.
   c. Security. The officers suggested in the covering letter accompanying this proposal are both at present stationed at Bursledon, where they frequently go sailing together; the Commando officer owns a double folbot which is used daily; there are MGBs stationed at Bursledon; training could therefore be started without delay without arousing any suspicions that an operation was under rehearsal.

Another cockpit view of the Fw 190A-3.

Pinckney's proposal was allocated the operational codename 'Airthief' and detailed planning began. Upon examination of the various alternatives, Cherbourg/Maupertus was thought to offer the best chance of success for the enterprise.

Yet, while 'Airthief' was still in the embryo stage, the operation was overtaken by a coincidence more bizarre than any fiction writer would dare present to a reader. On the same day that Pinckney submitted his proposal, 23 June 1942, an Fw 190 pilot became disorientated during a fight with Spitfires over southern England. After mistaking the Bristol Channel for the English Channel, the plane made a wheels-down landing on Pembrey airfield in South Wales. Thus the RAF received an example of the coveted German fighter without having to resort to 'Airthief'.

Philip Pinckney did not survive the war; he was killed in action in Italy in 1944. Discussing the chances of success of 'Airthief' with the author many years later, Jeffrey Quill commented:

'Provided we could get to the aircraft with its engine running, get the German airman out of the cockpit dead or alive and get me into it, I thought I had a 50-50 chance of getting back to England. As to the early part of the operation I was not qualified to have a view and I was guided entirely by Philip who seemed very confident and I would just have done what he said. He was obviously relying upon stealth – and perhaps we might have got away with it. Philip was always evasive about his own plans for getting back. I had a splendid way of getting back by air, but it was a very different kettle of fish for him. But he was very resourceful and might well have made it, one way or another, provided I had got the aircraft off the airfield without too much of a hue and cry.

'Anyway, it was a non-event as it turned out. Philip Pinckney was the inspiration behind the whole thing. Had it succeeded it would have been 90 per cent due to him and the balance of danger would have been heavily against him. I think he was bitterly disappointed when it was called off and he was quite cross about the German pilot landing in Wales. I am afraid I have to confess to a certain easing of tension within my guts!'

CHAPTER 5

UNSOLICITED TESTIMONIALS

'Captured Focke Wulf 190 will be flying in Green Area from 29/6 onwards from RAE Farnborough with or without Spitfire escort. All aircrews and gunners are to be warned that attacks should not, repeat, not, be made on Fw 190 aircraft in this area. Fw 190 will carry British markings.'
Secret teleprinter message from Headquarters Fighter Command to all air defence units, 29 June 1942.

The chance acquisition of the Focke Wulf 190A-3 sent a ripple of excitement running through Fighter Command. The aircraft and its performance were examined in the minutest detail, to derive anything of value from the windfall. At the same time the Commander in Chief of Fighter Command, Air Chief Marshal Sir William Sholto Douglas, wrote a strongly worded letter concerning the German fighter to the Under Secretary of State for Air, Lord Sherwood.

> MOST SECRET
> Headquarters, Fighter Command
> Royal Air Force
> Bentley Priory
> Stanmore
> Middlesex

FC/S. 2947
17th July, 1942

Sir,

I attach a memorandum on the performance and operational characteristics of day-fighters, with particular reference to what our position will be in the Spring of 1943 [not reproduced here]. I ask that immediate consideration should be given to the points raised in this memorandum.

1. It is scarcely necessary for me to emphasise the point that quality is more important than quantity in the production of fighters. At the beginning of the war our fighters possessed technical superiority over those of the enemy. We have gradually lost this lead and we are now in a position of inferiority. It is essential that this position should be remedied before next spring when it is anticipated that intensive air fighting will take place.

2. I seem to detect a spirit of complacency in the Ministry of Aircraft Production. This is borne out by the speeches of the Minister of Production and the Minister of Aircraft Production in the debate in the House of Commons on Tuesday, 14 July. They appear to find it difficult to believe that we have really lost our lead in fighter performance. There is however no doubt in my mind, nor in the minds of my fighter pilots, that the *Fw 190 is the best all-round fighter in the world today* [author's italics]. It is no answer to say that the position will be reversed when the Spitfire IX comes into general use. In the first place I have only fourteen Spitfire IXs, whereas the enemy has between two and three hundred Fw 190s. In several respects the Fw 190 is superior to the Spitfire IX, e.g. in climb and acceleration at certain critical altitudes and in negative G carburation. The most alarming aspect of the position however is that, whereas the Spitfire with Merlin engine is almost at the end of its possible development, the Fw 190 is only in the early stages of its development. Reports are already to hand of more horsepower being put into the engine of the Fw 190, and there is no doubt that with its greater engine capacity, it can in time easily outstrip the Merlin Spitfire in performance. This in fact is likely to have happened by next spring.

3. In my opinion therefore this is no time for complacency in regard to the quality and performance of our day-fighter aircraft. In the attached memorandum will be found certain suggestions for making the necessary improvements. These are the result of a study of the problem by my technical staff, who may not have all the facts and future possibilities at their fingertips. At the same time I ask that they should be given serious consideration.

I have the honour to be,

Sir,

Your obedient Servant,

(signed) W. S. Douglas

Air Chief Marshal

Air Officer Commanding-in-Chief
Fighter Command, Royal Air Force

The under Secretary of State
Air Ministry,
Whitehall, SW1

Time would reveal that Sir Sholto Douglas had been over-pessimistic in his view that improved versions of the Fw 190 would '. . . outstrip the Merlin Spitfire in performance'. In fact the Spitfire IX would be a worthy opponent for most versions of the Fw 190, and the Mark XIV would prove superior. Nevertheless, the letter reveals clearly that in the summer of 1942 the German fighter was a matter of considerable concern to the RAF commander.

Following initial flight trials at the Royal Aircraft Establishment at Farnborough in July 1942, the captured Focke Wulf 190 flew to the Air Fighting Development Unit at Duxford for tactical trials. The resultant report, issued in August 1942 and reproduced below almost in its entirety, is a model of what such an intelligence document should contain. In places the language was complimentary in the extreme. The reader should bear in mind that these are not the words of a Focke Wulf salesman trying to boost his firm's product, but those of an enemy forced to give an opponent grudging admiration in time of war.

The captured Fw 190A-3, works number 313, pictured at the RAF airfield at Pembrey shortly after its pilot landed there inadvertently on 23 June 1942.

Brief Description of the Aircraft

The Fw 190 is a small, compact, single-seater, single-engined, low wing monoplane fighter. There are fittings under the fuselage to enable it to carry bombs or a jettisonable fuel tank. It has a fully retractable undercarriage and partially retractable tailwheel. The mainplane is fully cantilever and is fitted with split flaps of metal construction. The flaps have four positions: retracted, 15° for take-off, 30° for use in the event of a balked landing, and fully down for landing. Operation is by means of three electric push buttons.

The power unit is a BMW 801-D, 14-cylinder, 2-row radial engine, fitted with a two-speed supercharger giving the best performance at 9,000 and 18,000 ft [2,745 and 5,490 m]. Between 5,000 and 8,000 ft [1,525 and 2,440 m] the performance of the engine falls off as it is just below the height where the two-speed supercharger comes into operation. The estimated power of the engine is 1,700 h.p. at the maximum power altitude of 18,000 ft. The engine oil coolers and induction system are totally enclosed by an extremely neat cowling and cooling is assisted by an engine driven fan behind the propeller.

The constant speed VDM 3-bladed metal propeller is electrically operated. It is automatically controlled by a hydraulic governor and, if required, manually by an electric switch on the pilot's throttle lever.

The undercarriage is retracted by pushing a red button. The operation for lowering the undercarriage consists of pushing a green button and releasing the undercarriage locks by pulling a lever which is situated on the left-hand side of the cockpit. In the event of an electrical failure, the only emergency method of lowering the undercarriage is by means of this lever, gravity completing the operation. The tailwheel is partially retracted and lowered mechanically by a cable attached to the starboard undercarriage leg. It is fully castoring and can be locked for take-off and landing by holding the control column right back.

All the control surfaces are fabric covered and are fitted with metal trimming tabs which can be adjusted only on the ground. For trimming, the tailplane is adjustable in flight over the range of +5° to -3°. It is operated electrically by two push buttons governing the up and down movements. There is a visual indicator in the cockpit.

The armament consists of 4 × 20 mm guns in the wing and 2 × 7.92 mm machine-guns in the engine cowling. The all-up weight of the aircraft, including pilot, is approximately 8,600 lb [3,900 kg] and the wing loading is 41.8 lb sq ft [3.88 kg/m^2].

PILOT'S COCKPIT

The cockpit is fully enclosed and although rather narrow is otherwise extremely comfortable. The pilot's position is excellent and as his feet are level with the seat, it enables him to withstand high acceleration forces without 'blacking-out'. The positioning of instruments is excellent and all controls fall easily to the pilot's hand, the absence of unnecessary levers and gadgets being particularly noticeable. The front panel is in two pieces, the top containing the primary flying and engine instruments and the lower panel the secondary instruments. Cut-out switches for the electrical circuits are housed in hinged flaps on the starboard side.

The switches and indicators for the operation of the undercarriage, flaps and tail incidence, are situated on the port side. The control column is the standard German fighter type with a selector switch and firing button for guns, and a send/receive button for the wireless.

The cockpit canopy, which is made of moulded plexiglas, is well shaped and extends far back along the fuselage. The bullet-proof windscreen has a pronounced slope which is unusual. The canopy can be slid back for entry and exit and for taxiing, operation being by means of a crank handle similar to that in the Westland Whirlwind. The enclosure can be jettisoned in an emergency by pressing a red lever on the starboard side; this unlocks the hood and detonates a cartridge which breaks the runners and blows the canopy off. Heating for the cockpit appears efficient, and cooling is effected by a small flap on the port side and seems quite sufficient for the pilot's comfort.

ARMOUR PLATE

The pilot's bucket seat is made of 8-mm armour plate and in the unprotected gaps behind are fitted shaped strips varying in thickness between 5 and 6 mm. The pilot's head and shoulders are protected by shaped armour plate 13 mm thick and the windscreen is of bullet-proof glass about 1¾ in thick. Both fuel tanks are self-sealing. The oil tank, which is situated in front of the engine cowling, is protected by a ring of armour plate varying in thickness, and the tank itself is surrounded by a toughened steel ring.

RADIO

The wireless installation is the old type FuG7 and the only unusual feature is that there is no wireless mast, there being instead a short aerial between the tail fin and the cockpit canopy.

OXYGEN

The aircraft is fitted with standard improved Hohenatem oxygen equipment with Blaser attachment, giving pure oxygen at high altitude. Three bottles of unusual shape are the source of supply. It was not possible to test the efficiency of this equipment but it is understood that the RAE are carrying out investigations and will render a report in due course.

COMPASS

A Patin Distant Reading Pilot's Compass is installed in the centre of the dashboard and the Master Unit is in the rear of the Fuselage. An aircraft silhouette takes the place of the normal needle and indicates the direction which the aircraft is flying. There is an adjustable verge ring which can be set to any desired course and the aircraft then turned until the silhouette is pointing to the course selected. The compass generally is of excellent design and the dial is situated in a position where it can be easily seen by the pilot. The magnet is many times more powerful than in our compasses, and as a result is less affected by northerly turning and acceleration errors. It is also unaffected by current or voltage fluctuations, or changes in temperature.

ARMAMENT CHARACTERISTICS

The armament consists of:

i. Two MG 17 guns of 7.92-mm calibre fitted above the engine, synchronised, firing through the propeller arc.

ii. Two MG 151/20 guns of 20-mm calibre, synchronised, firing through the propeller arc are installed in the wing roots about 12 in out from the engine cowling.

iii. Two Oerlikon FF 20-mm guns fitted in the wings outboard of the propeller arc.

GUN BUTTONS AND SWITCHES

The guns are fired by means of a button on the front of the control column. A small selector switch at the side of the column enables the pilot to select the following alternatives:

i. MG 17 and MG 151/20 guns.

ii. Oerlikon FF 20-mm guns.

iii. All guns.

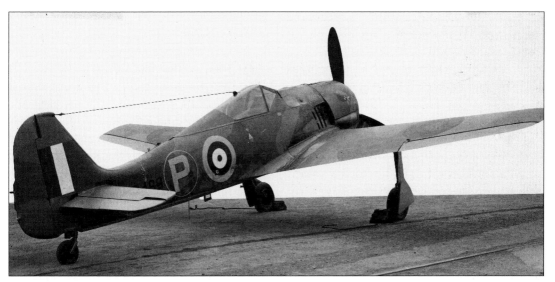

Finders keepers: the captured Fw 190A-3 pictured in the markings of its new owners.

In addition to this it is possible, by means of cut-out switches which are situated on the starboard side of the cockpit, to fire each pair of guns independently. There are ammunition counters in the cockpit for each gun.

HEATING
Hot air from the engine cowling is led by means of ducts to the ammunition chutes of the MG 17 guns and thence upwards to the breech mechanism. The Oerlikon FF 20-mm guns are also heated by hot air from the engine cowling. No special provision is made for heating the MG 151/20 guns and it is thought that owing to their position near the engine this is unnecessary.

SIGHT
A reflector sight, type Revi 12-D, is mounted 1½ in to starboard of the vertical centre line. The graticule is 5° 48' in diameter, which is the equivalent to approximately 95 m.p.h. for the high muzzle velocity of the German armament. Vertical and horizontal lines are marked off in degree steps from the centre of the graticule. Seven such lines are visible each way, these lines assist the pilot in range estimation and allowing for line.

HARMONIZATION
The harmonization ranges for each pair of guns are:

Two MG 17 guns at 300 metres or 330 yards.
Two MG 151/20 guns at 450 metres or 490 yards.
Two Oerlikon FF 20-mm guns at 250 metres or 270 yards.

The gun lines of the MG 17 guns are not symmetrical about the vertical centre line. The port gun converges whereas the starboard gun diverges with the result that they cross over 1 ft 2 in to starboard. This may be due to incorrect harmonization.

SIGHTING VIEW
The sighting view, when sitting comfortably in the normal position, is about half a ring [of deflection] better than that from a Spitfire. The view downwards from the centre of the sight graticule of the edge of the reflector plate holder is about 5 degrees. This view is not obtained by elevating the guns (and consequently the sight) relative to the line of flight, but is entirely due to the attitude of the aircraft in flight, which is nose down.

TACTICAL TRIALS

GENERAL
The Fw 190 is considered an excellent low and medium altitude fighter. It is fast, well armed and very manoeuvrable. The fighting qualities have been compared with a Spitfire VB, Spitfire IX, Mustang IA, Lockheed P-38F, Typhoon and the prototype Griffon-engined Spitfire. All aircraft were carrying full war load.

FLYING CHARACTERISTICS
The aircraft is pleasant to fly, all controls being extremely light and positive. The aircraft is difficult to taxi due to the excessive weight on the self-centring tailwheel when on the ground. For take-off, 15° of flap is required, and it is necessary to keep the control column back to avoid swinging during the initial stage of the take-off run. The run is approximately the same as that of the Spitfire IX.

Once airborne, the pilot immediately feels at home in the aircraft. The retraction of the flaps and undercarriage is barely noticeable although the aircraft will sink if the retraction of the flaps is made before a reasonably high airspeed has been obtained.

The stalling speed of the aircraft is high, being approximately 110 m.p.h. [177 k.m./h.]

with the undercarriage and flaps retracted, and 105 m.p.h. [169 k.m./h.] with the undercarriage and flaps fully down. All controls are effective up to the stall. One excellent feature of this aircraft is that it is seldom necessary to retrim under all conditions of flight.

The best approach speed for landing with flaps and undercarriage down is between 130 and 140 m.p.h. [209 and 225 k.m./h.] indicated, reducing to about 125 m.p.h. [201 k.m./h.] when crossing the edge of the aerodrome. Owing to the steep angle of glide, the view during the approach is good and the actual landing is straightforward, the touchdown occurring at approximately 110 m.p.h. The landing run is about the same as that of the Spitfire IX. The view on landing is poor due to the tail-down attitude of the aircraft. The locking of the tailwheel again assists in preventing swing during the landing run.

The aircraft is very pleasant for aerobatics even at high speed.

PERFORMANCE

The all-round performance of the Fw 190 is good. Only brief performance tests have been carried out and the figures obtained give a maximum speed of approximately 390 m.p.h. True at 1.42 atmospheres boost, 2,700 r.p.m. at the maximum power altitude of about 18,000 ft. All flights at maximum power were carried out for a duration of 2 minutes only.

There are indications that the engine of this aircraft is de-rated, this being supported by the pilot's instruction card found in the cockpit. Further performance tests and engine investigation are to be carried out by the RAE and more definite information will then be available.

Throughout the trials the engine has been running very roughly and as a result pilots flying the aircraft have little confidence in its reliability. The cause of this roughness has not yet been ascertained but it is thought that it may be due to a bad period of vibration at certain engine speeds which may also affect the injection system. [Later it was discovered that the roughness was due to fouling of the Bosch sparking plugs after a short period of running. The fault was cured by fitting Siemens type plugs taken from the BMW 801A engine of a crashed Do 217 bomber.]

ENDURANCE

The total of 115 gallons [522 l] of fuel is carried in two self-sealing tanks and each tank is fitted with an immersed fuel pump for use at altitude. A total of 9 gallons [40.8 l] of oil is carried in a protected oil tank. The approximate endurance under operational conditions, including dogfights and a climb to 25,000 ft [7,622 m] is approximately 1 hour 20 minutes. There is a red warning light fitted in a prominent position which illuminates when there is only sufficient fuel left for 20 minutes flying.

CLIMB

The rate of climb up to 18,000 ft [5,488 m] under maximum continuous climbing conditions at 1.35 atmospheres boost 2,450 r.p.m., 165 m.p.h. is between 3,000 and 3,250 ft/min [15.24 to 16.51 m/sec]. The initial rate of climb when pulling up from level flight at fast cruising speed is high and the angle steep, and from a dive is phenomenal. It is considered that the de-rated version of the Fw 190 is unlikely to be met above 25,000 ft [7,622 m] as the power of the engine starts falling off at 22,000 ft and by 25,000 ft has fallen off considerably. It is not possible to give the rate of climb at this altitude.

DIVE

The Fw 190 has a high rate of dive, the initial acceleration being excellent. The maximum

A close up of the canopy of the captured Fw 190. Royal Air Force officers were greatly impressed by the visibility from the pilot's position and the official report from the Air Fighting Development Unit stated: 'The view for searching from the Fw 190 is the best that has yet been seen by this unit.'

speed so far obtained in a dive is 580 m.p.h. [934 k.m./h.] True at 16,000 ft [4,880 m], and at this speed the controls, although slightly heavier, are still remarkably light. One very good feature is that no alteration of trim form level flight is required either during the entry or during the pull-out. Due to the fuel injection system it is possible to enter the dive by pushing the control column forward without the engine cutting.

SEARCH VIEW

The view for search from the Fw 190 is the best that has yet been seen by this Unit. The cockpit hood is of moulded plexiglas and offers an unrestricted view all round. No rear view mirror is fitted and it is considered unnecessary as the backward view is so good. The hood must not be opened in flight as it is

understood that tail buffeting may occur and that there is a chance of the hood being blown off. This, however, is not a disadvantage for day search as the quality of the plexiglas is excellent. During conditions of bad visibility and rain, or in the event of oil being thrown on the windscreen, the fact that the hood must not be opened in flight is obviously a disadvantage.

INSTRUMENT FLYING

The aircraft, although extremely light on all controls, is reasonably easy to fly on instruments. There are no artificial horizon or climb and dive indicators, which are naturally missed by British pilots. It appears that instrument flying is carried out by use of the gyro compass, turn and bank indicator, altimeter and air speed indicator.

LOW FLYING

The good all-round view from the aircraft, particularly over the nose, makes the Fw 190 very suitable for low flying and ground strafing. Another good point is that the sight is depressed, which would probably help in preventing pilots from flying into the ground. In conditions of bad visibility, however, low flying is likely to be unpleasant as the hood must not be opened in flight.

FORMATION FLYING

The aircraft is easy to fly in formation and due to the good view, all types of formation can be flown without difficulty. The aircraft has a wide speed range which greatly assists in regaining formation, but care must be taken to avoid over-shooting as its clean lines make deceleration slow.

NIGHT FLYING

The aircraft was not flown at night but was inspected with the engine running on a dark night, with no moon. The cockpit lighting appeared very efficient and did not reflect on the canopy. The exhaust flames viewed from about 100 yards ahead were seen as a dull red halo, and viewed from the beam could be seen from about 500 yards away. The flame can be seen from astern 200 yards away. It is considered that the glare will badly affect the pilot, particularly during take-off and landing. Although the aircraft carried full night-flying equipment, there is no indication that flame dampers are normally fitted. It is possible that the cause of the red flame may be due to faulty mixture.

ENGINE STARTING AND QUICK TAKE-OFFS

It is possible to start the engine by means of the internal battery, or an external battery, and in the event of emergency by hand. The method of starting is similar to the Me 109,

being an inertia system. If the engine is cold it will require running for a considerable time before the oil temperature reaches the safety level for take-off and even with a warm engine some minutes are necessary as the cooling is so effective on the ground. This is obviously a disadvantage and coupled with the fact that the aircraft is not easy to taxi, makes the Fw 190 inferior to our aircraft for quick take-offs.

FIGHTING QUALITIES

The fighting qualities of the Fw 190 have been compared with various aircraft, and each comparison is dealt with separately. The trials against the Griffon Spitfire were only brief and against the Typhoon had to be abandoned before completion owing to the unsatisfactory state of the engine of the Fw 190.

FW 190 VERSUS SPITFIRE VB

The Fw 190 was compared with a Spitfire VB from an operational squadron for speed and all-round manoeuvrability at heights up to 25,000 ft. The Fw 190 is superior in speed at all heights, and the approximate differences are as follows:

At 2,000 ft [610 m] the Fw 190 is 25–30 m.p.h. [40–48 k.m./h.] faster than the Spitfire VB.

At 3,000 ft [915 m] the Fw 190 is 30–35 m.p.h. [48–56 k.m./h.] faster than the Spitfire VB.

At 5,000 ft [1,525 m] the Fw 190 is 25 m.p.h. faster than the Spitfire VB.

At 9,000 ft [2,744 m] the Fw 190 is 25–30 m.p.h. faster than the Spitfire VB.

At 15,000 ft [4,573 m] the Fw 190 is 20 m.p.h. [32 k.m./h.] faster than the Spitfire VB.

At 18,000 ft [5,488 m] the Fw 190 is 20 m.p.h. faster than the Spitfire VB.

At 21,000 ft the Fw 190 [6,400 m] is 20–25 m.p.h. faster than the Spitfire VB.

The comparative trial confirmed that the Spitfire VB was inferior to the Fw 190 in almost all aspects of combat performance.

CLIMB

The climb of the Fw 190 is superior to that of the Spitfire VB at all heights. The best speeds for climbing are approximately the same, but the angle of the Fw 190 is considerably steeper. Under maximum continuous climbing conditions the climb of the Fw 190 is about 450 ft/min better up to 25,000 feet [7,620 m]. With both aircraft flying at high cruising speed and then

pulling up into a climb, the superior climb of the Fw 190 is even more marked. When both aircraft are pulled into a climb from a dive, the Fw 190 draws away very rapidly and the pilot of the Spitfire has no hope of catching it.

DIVE

Comparative dives between the two aircraft have shown that the Fw 190 can leave the

Spitfire with ease, particularly during the initial stages.

MANOEUVRABILITY

The manoeuvrability of the Fw 190 is better than that of the Spitfire VB except in turning circles, when the Spitfire can quite easily out-turn it. The Fw 190 has better acceleration under all conditions of flight and this must obviously be useful during combat.

When the Fw 190 was in a turn and was attacked by the Spitfire, the superior rate of roll enabled it to flick into a diving turn in the opposite direction. The pilot of the Spitfire found great difficulty in following this manoeuvre and even when prepared for it was seldom able to allow the correct deflection. A dive from this manoeuvre enabled the Fw 190 to draw away from the Spitfire which was then forced to break off the attack.

Several flights were carried out to ascertain the best evasive manoeuvres to adopt if 'bounced'. It was found that if the Spitfire was cruising at low speed and was 'bounced' by the Fw 190, it was easily caught even if the Fw 190 was sighted when well out of range, and the Spitfire was then forced to take avoiding action by using its superiority in turning circles. If on the other hand the Spitfire was flying at maximum continuous cruising and was 'bounced' under the same conditions, it has a reasonable chance of avoiding being caught by opening the throttle and going into a shallow dive, provided the Fw 190 was seen in time. This forced the Fw 190 into a stern chase and although it eventually caught the Spitfire, it took some time and as a result was drawn a considerable distance away from its base. This is a particularly useful method of evasion for the Spitfire if it is 'bounced' when returning from a sweep. This manoeuvre has been carried out during recent operations and has been successful on several occasions.

If the Spitfire VB is 'bounced' it is thought unwise to evade by diving steeply, as the Fw 190 will have little difficulty in catching up owing to its superiority in the dive.

The above trials have shown that the Spitfire VB must cruise at high speed when in an area where enemy fighters can be expected. It will, then, in addition to lessening the chances of being successfully 'bounced', have a better chance of catching the Fw 190, particularly if it has the advantage of surprise.

Fw 190 versus Spitfire IX

The Focke Wulf 190 was compared with a fully operational Spitfire IX for speed and manoeuvrability at heights up to 25,000 ft. The Spitfire IX at most heights is slightly superior in speed to the Fw 190 and the approximate differences in speeds at various heights are as follows:

At 2,000 ft [610 m] the Fw 190 is 7–8 m.p.h. [11–13 k.m./h.] faster than the Spitfire IX.

At 5,000 ft [1,524 m] the Fw 190 and the Spitfire IX are approximately the same.

At 8,000 ft [2,440 m] the Spitfire IX is 8 m.p.h. faster than the Fw 190.

At 15,000 ft [4,573 m] the Spitfire IX is 5 m.p.h. [8 k.m./h.] faster than the Fw 190.

At 18,000 ft [5,488 m] the Fw 190 is 3 m.p.h. faster than the Spitfire IX.

At 21,000 ft [6,400 m] the Fw 190 and the Spitfire IX are approximately the same.

At 25,000 ft [7,620 m] the Spitfire IX is 5–7 m.p.h. faster than the Fw 190.

CLIMB

During comparative climbs at various heights up to 23,000 ft, with both aircraft flying under maximum continuous climbing conditions, little difference was found

During the trial the Spitfire IX was shown to have a performance similar to that of the Fw 190A-3.

between the two aircraft although on the whole the Spitfire IX was slightly better. Above 22,000 ft the climb of the Fw 190 is falling off rapidly, whereas the climb of the Spitfire IX is increasing. When both aircraft were flying at a high cruising speed and were pulled up into a climb from level flight, the Fw 190 had a slight advantage in the initial stages of the climb due to its better acceleration. This superiority was slightly increased when both aircraft were pulled up into the climb from the dive.

It must be appreciated that the differences between the two aircraft are only slight and that in actual combat the advantage in climb will be with the aircraft that has the initiative.

DIVE

The Fw 190 is faster than the Spitfire IX in a dive, particularly during the initial stage. This superiority is not so marked as with the Spitfire VB.

MANOEUVRABILITY

The Fw 190 is more manoeuvrable than the Spitfire IX except in turning circle, when it is out-turned without difficulty.

The superior rate of roll of the Fw 190 enabled it to avoid the Spitfire IX if attacked when in a turn by flicking over into a diving turn in the opposite direction, and as with the Spitfire VB, the Spitfire IX had great difficulty in following this manoeuvre. It would have been easier for the Spitfire IX to follow the Fw 190 in a diving turn if its engine had been fitted with a negative 'G' carburettor, as this type of engine with the ordinary carburettor cuts very easily.

The Spitfire IX's worst heights for fighting the Fw 190 are between 18,000 and 22,000 ft [5,488 and 6,707 m] and below 3,000 ft [915 m]. At these heights the Fw 190 is a little faster.

Both aircraft 'bounced' one another in order to ascertain the best evasive tactics to adopt. The Spitfire IX could not be caught when 'bounced' if it was cruising at high speed and saw the Fw 190 when well out of range. When the Spitfire IX was cruising at low speed its inferiority in acceleration gave the Fw 190 a reasonable chance of catching it up and the same applied if the position was reversed and the Fw 190 was 'bounced' by the Spitfire IX, except that overtaking took a little longer.

The initial acceleration of the Fw 190 is better than the Spitfire IX under all conditions of flight, except in level flight at such altitudes where the Spitfire has a speed advantage and then, providing the Spitfire is cruising at high speed, there is little to choose between the two aircraft.

The general impression gained by pilots taking part in the trials is that the Spitfire IX compares favourably with the Fw 190 and that provided the Spitfire has the initiative, it has undoubtedly a good chance of shooting the Fw 190 down.

FW 190 VERSUS MUSTANG 1A (P-51A)

The Fw 190 was compared with a fully operational Mustang 1A for speed and all-round performance up to 23,000 ft [7,010 m]. There was little to choose between the aircraft in speed at all heights except between 10,000 and 15,000 ft [3,050 and 4,573 m], where the Mustang was appreciably faster. Approximate differences were as follows:

At 2,000 ft [610 m] the Fw 190 is 2 m.p.h. [3 k.m./h.] faster than the Mustang 1A.

At 5,000 ft [1,525 m] the Mustang is 5 m.p.h. [8 k.m./h.] faster than the Fw 190.

At 10,000 ft [3,050 m] the Mustang is 15 m.p.h. [24 k.m./h.] faster than the Fw 190.

At 20,000 ft [6,100 m] the Fw 190 is 5 m.p.h. faster than the Mustang 1A.

At 23,000 ft [7,010 m] the Fw 190 is 5 m.p.h. faster than the Mustang 1A.

CLIMB

The climb of the Fw 190 is superior to that of the Mustang 1A at all heights. The best climbing speed for the Mustang is approximately 10 m.p.h. [16 k.m./h.] slower than that for the Fw 190; the angle is not nearly so steep and the rate of climb is considerably inferior. When both aircraft are pulled up into a climb after a fast dive, the inferiority in the initial stage of the climb is not so marked, but if the climb is continued the Fw 190 draws away rapidly.

DIVE

Comparative dives have shown that there is little to choose between the two aircraft and if anything the Mustang is slightly faster in a prolonged dive.

MANOEUVRABILITY

The manoeuvrability of the Fw 190 is better than that of the Mustang except in turning circles where the Mustang is superior. In the rolling plane at high speed the Mustang compares more favourably with the Fw 190 than does the Spitfire.

The acceleration of the Fw 190 under all conditions of flight is slightly better than that of the Mustang and this becomes more marked when both aircraft are cruising at low speed.

When the Fw 190 was attacked by the Mustang in a turn, the usual manoeuvre of flicking into a diving turn in the opposite direction was not so effective against the Mustang as against the Spitfire, particularly if the aircraft were flying at high speed. The fact that the engine of the Mustang does not cut during the application of negative 'G' proved a great asset and gave the Mustang a reasonable chance of following the Fw 190 and shooting it down. It must be appreciated, however, that much depends on which aircraft has the initiative and that obviously

the Fw 190 can escape if the Mustang is seen well out of range. The Fw 190 in this case will almost certainly utilise its superior climb.

Trials were carried out to ascertain the best manoeuvre to adopt when 'bounced'. If the Mustang was cruising at high speed and saw the Fw 190 about 2,000 yards away, it usually managed to avoid it by opening up to full throttle and diving away, and once speed had been built up it was almost impossible for the Fw 190 to catch it. When the Mustang was 'bounced' by the Fw 190 when flying slowly, it was unable to get away by diving and was forced to evade by means of a quick turn as the Fw 190 came into firing range.

When the Fw 190 was 'bounced' by the Mustang, it could evade by using its superiority in the rolling plane and then pull up violently from the resultant dive into a steep climb which left the Mustang behind. If the Mustang is not seen until it is fairly close, it will get the chance of a short burst before it is out-climbed.

Against the Fw 190 the worst heights for the Mustang IA were above 20,000 ft [6,100 m] and below 3,000 ft [915 m] where the Fw 190 is slightly superior in speed. The best height for the Mustang was found to be between 5,000 and 15,000 ft [1,525 and 4,573 m].

FW 190 VERSUS LOCKHEED P-38F LIGHTNING

The Fw 190 was compared with an operationally equipped P-38F flown by an experienced US Army Air Force pilot. The two aircraft were compared for speed and all-round manoeuvrability at heights up to 23,000 ft [7,010 m]. The Fw 190 was superior in speed at all heights up to 22,000 ft [6,710 m] where the two aircraft were approximately the same. The difference in speed decreases as the P-38F gains altitude, until at 23,000 ft it is slightly faster. The approximate differences in speeds are as follows:

At 2,000 ft [610 m] the Fw 190 is 15 m.p.h. [24 k.m./h.] faster than the P-38F.
At 8,000 ft [2,440 m] the Fw 190 is 15 m.p.h. faster than the P-38F.
At 15,000 ft [4,573 m] the Fw 190 is 5–8 m.p.h. [8–13 k.m./h.] faster than the P-38F.
At 23,000 ft [7,010 m] the P-38F is 6–8 m.p.h. [9–13 k.m./h.] faster than the Fw 190.

CLIMB

The climb of the P-38F is not as good as that of the Fw 190 up to 15,000 ft. Above this height the climb of the P-38F improves rapidly until at 20,000 ft [6,010 m] it becomes superior. The best climbing speed for the P-38F is about 20 m.p.h. [32 k.m./h.] less than that of the Fw 190 and the angle is approximately the same. The initial rate of climb of the Fw 190 either from level flight or a dive is superior to that of the P-38F at all heights below 20,000 ft and above this height the climb of the P-38F becomes increasingly better.

DIVE

Comparative dives between the two aircraft proved the Fw 190 to be better, particularly in the initial stage. During prolonged dives the P-38F on occasion was catching up slightly with the Fw 190, but during actual combat it is unlikely that the P-38F would have time to catch up before having to break off the attack.

MANOEUVRABILITY

The Fw 190 is superior to that of the P-38F, particularly in the rolling plane. Although at high speed the Fw 190 is superior in turning circles, it can be out-turned if the P-38F reduces its speed to about 140 m.p.h. [225 k.m./h.], at which speed it can carry out a very tight turn which the Fw 190 cannot follow.

The acceleration of the two aircraft was compared and the Fw 190 was found to be better in all respects.

When the Fw 190 'bounced' the P-38F and was seen when over 1,000 yards away, the pilot's best manoeuvre was to go into a diving turn and if it found the Fw 190 was catching it up, to pull up into a spiral climb, flying at its lowest possible speed. Although time did not permit trials to be carried out with the Fw 190 being 'bounced' by the P-38F, it is thought that the P-38F would stand a reasonable chance of shooting down the Fw 190 provided it had a slight height advantage and the element of surprise. If the pilot of the Fw 190 sees the P-38F when it is just out of range, a quick turn in one direction followed by a diving turn in the opposite direction will give the P-38F a most difficult target, and as the acceleration and speed of the Fw 190 in a dive builds up very rapidly, it is likely to be able to dive away out of range.

FW 190 VERSUS 4-CANNON TYPHOON

Owing to the unsatisfactory condition of the engine of the Fw 190 which caused the trials to be abandoned, only brief tests could be carried out against the Typhoon. Arrangements have been made with the RAE Farnborough to complete the trials as soon as the engine of the Fw 190 has been overhauled and passed fit for further flights. Trials were carried out against two operationally equipped Typhoons, one from a squadron and the other from the Hawker Aircraft Company. Both aircraft were flown by experienced pilots.

The Fw 190 was compared with the Typhoon for speed and all-round manoeuvrability at 2,000 ft [610 m] and in addition a partial climb was carried out between 12,000 and 17,000 ft [3,658 and 5,183 m]. At 2,000 ft there was little to choose between the two aircraft, the Typhoon being slightly faster. The runs were made from cruising speed at full throttle for a period of two minutes and this did not give the Typhoon time to build up to its maximum speed. From the knowledge of both aircraft it can be safely assumed that the Typhoon will be faster than the Fw 190 at all heights, having the best advantage in speed at the following approximate heights: 8,000, 10,000, 16,300 and 20,500 ft [2,440, 3,050, 4,970 and 6,250 m].

CLIMB

During the partial climb from 12,000 to 17,000 ft, the Typhoon was out-climbed by the Fw 190 quite easily. The best climbing speed of the Typhoon is considerably higher than of the Fw 190 and the angle not nearly so steep, the rate of climb at all heights being inferior. The difference in a comparative climb after a dive is unlikely to be so great.

DIVE

It is thought that the Typhoon will out-dive the Fw 190, but the Fw 190 is likely to be slightly better in the initial stage. The controls of the Typhoon, although good in a dive, are not so light and responsive as those of the Fw 190.

MANOEUVRABILITY

The manoeuvrability of the Fw 190 and the Typhoon was compared during one flight at 2,000 ft [610 m], the Typhoon being flown by a very experienced test pilot from Hawkers, and it appeared that there was little to choose between the two aircraft in turning circles. The opinion of both pilots was that it was doubtful whether either aircraft would be able to hold its sights on sufficiently long for accurate sighting. It should be borne in mind, however, that the pilot of the Fw 190 was reluctant at the time to risk stalling the aircraft in the turn at such a low height, and it is therefore possible that the turn could have been made tighter. The Typhoon was unable to follow the Fw 190 from a turn in one direction into a diving turn in the opposite direction due to the Fw 190's superiority in the rolling plane. The initial acceleration of the Typhoon, particularly from slow speed, is much slower although the difference in acceleration when flying at high speed is not so great. It is considered that the Fw 190 would have the greatest difficulty in 'bouncing' providing the Typhoon was flying at high speed. The Typhoon, however, should have a good chance of 'bouncing' the Fw 190 provided it has a slight height advantage.

FW 190 VERSUS GRIFFON SPITFIRE

[Variant later went into service as the Spitfire XII.] Two brief flights at between 1,000 and 2,000 ft [305 and 610 m] were carried out between the Fw 190 and the prototype Griffon Spitfire flown by an experienced test pilot from Messrs Vickers. Two speed runs were made from high cruising speed over a distance of about 10 miles [16 km]. The acceleration of the Spitfire proved superior to that of the Fw 190 and its speed appreciably faster. Owing to adverse weather conditions it was not possible to compare the two aircraft for dive and climb.

MANOEUVRABILITY

Brief manoeuvrability tests were carried out and the Spitfire had no difficulty in out-turning the Fw 190. It again should be borne in mind, however, that the pilot of the Fw 190 was reluctant at the time to risk stalling the aircraft in the turn at such a low height and it is therefore possible that the turn could have been tighter and the difference between them less marked.

CONCLUSIONS

The Fw 190 is undoubtedly a formidable low and medium altitude fighter.

Its designer has obviously given much thought to the pilot. The cockpit is extremely well laid out and the absence of large levers and unnecessary gadgets most noticeable. The pilot is given a comfortable seating position, and is well protected by armour.

The simplicity of the aircraft as a whole is an excellent feature, and enables new pilots to be thoroughly conversant with all controls in a very brief period.

The rough running of the engine is much disliked by all pilots and must be a great disadvantage, as lack of confidence in an engine makes flying over bad country or water most unpleasant.

The armament is good and well positioned, and the ammunition capacity should be sufficient for any normal fighter operation. The sighting view is approximately half a ring [of deflection] better than that from the Spitfire.

The all-round search view is the best that has yet been seen from any aircraft flown by this unit.

The flying characteristics are exceptional and a pilot new to the type feels at home within the first few minutes of flight. The controls are light and well-harmonised and all manoeuvres can be carried out without difficulty at all speeds. The fact that the Fw 190 does not require re-trimming under all conditions of flight is a particularly good point. The initial acceleration is very good and is particularly noticeable in the initial stages of a climb or dive. Perhaps one of the most outstanding qualities of this aircraft is the remarkable aileron control. It is possible to change from a turn in one direction to a turn in the opposite direction with incredible speed, and when viewed from another aircraft the change appears just as if a flick half-roll has been made.

It is considered that night flying would be unpleasant, particularly for landing and take-off, due to the exhaust glare and the fact that the cockpit canopy cannot be opened in flight.

The engine is easy to start but requires running up for a considerable time, even when warm, before the oil temperature reaches the safety level for take-off, and this coupled with the fact that the aircraft is not easy to taxi makes the Fw 190 inferior to our aircraft for quick take-offs.

The comparative fighting qualities of the Fw 190 have been compared with the Spitfire VB, Spitfire IX, Mustang IA, Lockheed P-38F, 4-cannon Typhoon and prototype Griffon Spitfire, all aircraft being flown by experienced pilots. The main conclusion gained from the tactical trials of the Fw 190 is that our fighter aircraft must fly at high speed when in an area where the Fw 190 is likely to be met. This will give our pilots the chance of 'bouncing' and catching the Fw 190 and, if 'bounced' themselves, the best chance of avoiding being shot down.

The all-round search view from the Fw 190 being exceptionally good makes it rather difficult to achieve the element of surprise. Here again, however, the advantage of our aircraft flying at high speed must not be overlooked, as they may even if seen by the pilot of the Fw 190 catch it before it has time to dive away.

CHAPTER 6

UNITS EQUIPPED WITH FW 190S 27 JULY 1942

LUFTFLOTTE 3 (FRANCE, BELGIUM)

Unit	Total	Serviceable
Jagdgeschwader 2		
Stab	4	3
I. Gruppe	36	29
II. Gruppe	37	34
III. Gruppe	39	31
10. Staffel	15	11[1]
Jagdgeschwader 26		
Stab	4	4
I. Gruppe	38	28
II. Gruppe	41	36
III. Gruppe	36	33
10. Staffel	15	12[1]
Aufklärungsgruppe 33		
1. Staffel	1	0[2]
Aufklärungsgruppe 123		
1. Staffel	1	0[3]

NOTES

1. Fighter-bomber unit.
2. Reconnaissance unit, also operated Bf 109s and Ju 88s.
3. Reconnaissance unit also operated Bf 110s and Ju 88s.

The death of an Fw 190. Although the Fw 190 had a better performance than the Mark V Spitfires confronting it on the Channel coast, the new German fighter was of course vulnerable to surprise attack. This remarkable series of photographs was taken by Flight Sergeant A. Robson, a New Zealander flying Spitfires with No. 485 Squadron, during a combat near Ambeletuese on the afternoon of 4 May 1942. Afterwards Robson reported: 'Flying as Blue 3 at 17,000 ft I saw two Fw 190s 2,000 ft below. Blue 1 dived to attack and I followed him. I fired two short bursts at one. He turned inland and I followed him to close range and fired the rest of my ammunition at him. I saw several hits. One wheel came down, the hood and pilot's helmet blew off. The enemy aircraft when last seen was flying with the starboard wing down at about 2,000 ft.' Robson, who obviously did not see the pilot bailing out, afterwards claimed one enemy aircraft 'probably destroyed'. The Fw 190 almost certainly belonged to *JG 2*.

LUFTFLOTTE 5 (ARCTIC SECTOR, EASTERN FRONT)

Unit	Total	Serviceable
Jagdgeschwader 5		
I. Gruppe	35	28
IV. Gruppe	26	20

LUFTWAFFENBEFELSHABER MITTE (REICH AIR DEFENCE)

Unit	Total	Serviceable
Jagdgeschwader 1		
Stab	4	4
I. Gruppe	37	34
II. Gruppe	38	28
III. Gruppe	40	33
IV. Gruppe	39	28

CHAPTER 7

IN ACTION AGAINST USAAF HEAVY BOMBERS

In the autumn of 1942 the US Eighth Air Force based in Britain began sending increasingly large formations of B-17s and B-24s to attack targets in occupied Europe. The German fighter pilots sent up to engage these heavy bombers found them tough opponents. Even battle-hardened pilots were unnerved by the powerful defensive crossfire.

On 9 October a force of 108 B-17s and B-24s with fighter escort attacked the Fives-Lille steel works in Belgium. Oberleutnant Otto Stammberger of *III./JG 26* was one of the Fw 190 pilots sent into action on that day; later he wrote:

'We attacked the enemy bombers in pairs, going in with great bravado: closing in fast from behind with throttles wide open, then letting fly. But at first the attacks were broken off much too early – as those great "barns" grew larger and larger our people were afraid of colliding with them. I wondered why I had scored no hits but then I considered the size of the things: 40 metres span! The next time I went in I thought: get in much closer, keep going, keep going. Then I opened fire, starting with his motors on the port wing. By the third such firing run the two port engines were burning well, and I had shot the starboard outer engine to smithereens. The enemy "kite" went down in wide spiralling left-hand turns, and crashed just east of Vendeville; four or five of the crew bailed out.'

Stammberger's narrative highlights the difficulty of engaging these bombers, and the huge amount of punishment they could take. The German pilot was fortunate in that the B-17 he went after had become separated from its formation, allowing him to make three deliberate attacks. Attacking bombers in formation was a much more difficult business. That day defending fighters shot down four heavy bombers, for a loss of two of their number.

The Fw 190 carried sufficient 20-mm ammunition for only 15 seconds' firing, and pilots had strict orders not to open fire at ranges greater than 400 metres. Fighter ace Major Anton Hackl, who flew Fw 190s for a time with *JG 11* in this role, outlined the problem to the author: 'If one came in from the rear there was a long period, closing from 1,000 metres to our firing range of 400 metres, when the bombers were firing at us but we could not fire at them. This was a very dangerous time and we lost a lot of aircraft trying to attack that way.'

When US heavy bombers made their first attacks on Germany, early in 1943, *Jagdgeschwader 1* was the sole day-fighter *Geschwader* defending the homeland. Its *Stab* and *II.*, *III.* and *IV. Gruppen* were wholly or partially equipped with the Fw 190. The unit's Focke Wulfs carried unusual markings. (*Above*) Black and white checkerboard cowling, with the marking of *2. Staffel*.

Face marking on the engine cowling of an Fw 190 of *II. Gruppe*.

'Fw 190 and Nutcracker' badge, believed to be carried by an aircraft of *Stab/JG 1*.

Even when the German pilot started firing on a heavy bomber, initially his fighter lacked the firepower necessary to give a good chance of shooting it down. The Fw 190A-4, the most effective single-engined fighter then available for this purpose, carried four 20-mm cannon and two 7.9-mm machine-guns. In a three-second burst it loosed off 130 rounds of 20-mm ammunition (fire from the 7.9-mm weapons was irrelevant in this sort of engagement). From the examination of crashed US bombers brought down by fighters, Luftwaffe officers found that few had less than twenty hits from 20-mm rounds. However, examination of combat films revealed that a pilot of average ability scored hits with only about 2 per cent of the carefully aimed rounds he fired. On those figures, an average pilot had to loose off *one thousand* rounds of 20-mm ammunition at the bomber to obtain the required twenty hits. But the Fw 190A-4's magazines carried only 500 rounds of 20-mm ammunition. Thus to secure the destruction of a heavy bomber it was necessary for two or more fighters to attack it. It is stressed that these figures relate to pilots of *average* shooting ability. Ace German pilots scored a much higher proportion of hits with the rounds they fired, while below average pilots scored even less.

HEAD-ON ATTACKS

Major Egon Mayer, the commander of III./ *JG 2*, experimented with head-on attacks on

Striking back at their tormentors: bombs falling from B-17 Fortresses on 26 April 1943, when 107 of these heavy bombers attacked the Focke Wulf works at Bremen. *Jagdgeschwader 1* fought a ferocious battle with the raiders and shot down fifteen bombers for a loss of five fighters destroyed and five more damaged. USAF

Two outstanding Fw 190 aces: Oberstleutnant Egon Mayer, left, and Hauptmann Hubertus von Bonin. Mayer developed the head-on attack tactic against US heavy bombers, and later commanded *JG 2*. He was credited with 102 victories in the west, including twenty-five four-engined bombers, before he was killed in a dogfight with P-47s in March 1944. Hubertus von Bonin rose to command *JG 54* and was holding that post when he was shot down and killed over Russia in December 1943.

the American formations as a means of overcoming this problem. In the forward hemisphere a bomber's crossfire was far less dangerous, and the 'fire-swept' zone could be crossed far more quickly. Moreover, the positioning of the bombers' armour gave little protection against head-on attacks. So fewer hits – as few as four or five with 20-mm rounds – were needed to inflict fatal damage.

On 23 November 1942 a force of 36 B-17s and B-24s, without fighter escort, attacked the U-boat base at St Nazaire on the west coast of France. Mayer led his *Gruppe* in a head-on attack on the heavy bombers and shot down three B-17s and seriously damaged one more. It was the most successful defensive effort by a single *Gruppe*, and other units copied the tactic.

There were problems with the head-on attack, however. The closing speed of the two formations was nearly 500 m.p.h., or 200 yards per second. That left time for only a brief half-second burst from 500 yards, before the German pilot had to break sharply away to avoid colliding with his victim. Using this method, a few ace pilots began to amass impressive scores against the heavy bombers. Anton Hackl commented, 'One accurate half-second burst from head-on and a [heavy bomber] kill was guaranteed. Guaranteed!'

Anton Hackl achieved a formidable reputation as a combat pilot, and by the end of the war he was credited with a total of 192 victories. Of those, thirty-two were heavy bombers and most were shot down in head-on attacks.

Yet it took considerable flying and shooting skill to deliver such an attack effectively. The less able pilots often failed to get their gunsight on the target, in the short time available before they had to break away. On the other hand, a head-on attack by a *Staffel* of fighters had a good chance of inflicting damage on one or two bombers so

they were forced to leave formation. Heavy bombers flying alone could then be finished off at leisure.

In the spring and summer of 1943 the Luftwaffe experimented with firing Wgr 21 unguided rockets into US formations from outside the range of the bombers' defensive fire. Again, the intention was to damage aircraft and force them to leave formation, so they could be picked off individually. Had the Wgr 21 been fitted with a proximity fuse, to detonate the warhead as it passed close to the target, it would have made all the difference to the weapon's effectiveness. But the German scientists had yet to overcome the formidable technical problems associated with this device. Instead, a time fuse detonated the warhead at a pre-set time after launch. However, pilots found it very hard to judge the firing range to the required limits. As a result most of these rockets detonated short of the target, or beyond it. Although they achieved a few spectacular successes, in general the rockets achieved little.

Also in the spring of 1943, the Fw 190A-5 entered production. This variant had the engine mounting lengthened by 15 cm (just under 6 in) to give improved handling. A few months later it was superseded by the A-6, with heavier armour and fast-firing MG 151 weapons in place of the MG/FF 20-mm cannon in the outer wing positions. Towards the end of 1943 the Fw 190A-7 entered production, with 13-mm Rheinmetall MG 131 heavy machine-guns replacing the 7.9-mm weapons above the engine. The Fw 190A-8, produced in greater numbers than any other version of the famous fighter, had several detailed improvements over the A-7.

In the spring of 1944 the increasing strength, reach and performance of the American escort fighters led to a further change in tactics. German fighter units assembled into large attack formations

HEAD-ON ATTACK ON A B-17

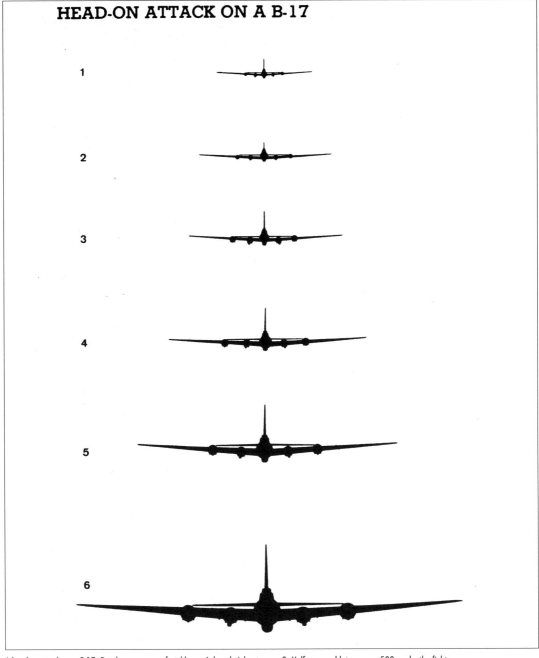

1

2

3

4

5

6

A head-on attack on a B-17. Put the page a comfortable arm's length (about 2 feet) in front of your eyes to see the apparent size of a B-17 at the various ranges. The two aircraft were closing on each other at about 500 m.p.h., or more than 200 yards per second.

1. Range 800 yards. If the bomber was to be hit, by this time it had to be centred in the fighter's gunsight graticule.

2. One second later, range 600 yards, fighter about to open fire.

3. Half a second later, range 500 yards, the fighter commenced firing.

4. Half a second later, range 400 yards, the fighter ceased firing.

5. Half a second later, range 300 yards, the fighter pilot eased up his nose to move out of the path of the bomber.

6. Half a second later, range 200 yards. If the fighter had not moved out of the bomber's path by now, a collision was almost inevitable.

Major Anton Hackl, another leading exponent of the head-on mode of attack, receiving the *Ritterkreuz* with Oak Leaves for leading fighter units in the defence of the homeland. Hackl survived the war, credited with a total 192 victories, of which 87 were in the West; he himself was shot down eight times. At various times he commanded *III./JG 11*, *II./JG 26*, *Jagdgeschwader 300* and *Jagdgeschwader 11*. Hackl

Major Josef 'Sepp' Wurmheller was credited with 102 victories of which 93 were in the west. He commanded first the *9. Staffel* of *JG 2*, later the *III. Gruppe*. He was killed on 22 June 1944 during a dogfight over France, when he collided with his wingman.

The tail of 'Sepp' Wurmheller's aircraft showing a score of seventy-three victories. The German ace reached that score early in 1943.

comprising three or four *Gruppen*, sometimes with more than a hundred fighters. These were vectored into position to deliver powerful head-on attacks on the bomber formations.

Yet when they engaged the enemy the German home defence fighter units found themselves in a Catch 22 situation. If their aircraft carried sufficient firepower to give a good chance of destroying an American heavy bomber, it was too heavy and too unwieldy to survive attacks from the American escorts. If the armament was reduced so that the fighter could dogfight with the escorts, it could not engage the bombers with much chance of success.

Oberleutnant Adolf Glunz spent most of his career with *II./JG 26* and was credited with seventy-one victories, all but three of which were in the west. He survived the war. via Girbig

An Fw 190 closes in to finish off a B-17 Fortress which had previously been hit and forced to leave the formation. The incident occurred immediately after the attack on the Focke Wulf factory at Oschersleben on 11 January 1944. During this action the US 8th Air Force lost sixty heavy bombers, one of the heaviest losses suffered by the force during the war. USAF

The appearance of the strongly built American bombers over Germany led to demands for more powerfully armed fighters for the home defence units. Among the armament combinations tried out in combat were six 20-mm cannon and two 30-mm MK103 cannon mounted externally under the wings in place of the outer wing 20-mm guns. VFW-Fokker

German civilians look over a B-17F of the 100th Bomb Group which crash-landed with battle damage near Freiburg in the autumn of 1943. via Schliephake

During the great day and night battles over Germany, the Luftwaffe directed its fighters into action from massive concrete operations bunkers such as this one near Grove in central Denmark. The top of the carefully camouflaged bunker was about 18 metres (nearly 60 ft) high and it had a bombproof roof 5 m (16 ft) thick.

An artist's impression of the scene inside the command post when the battle was being fought. The layout resembled a cinema, with the main air situation map on the right of the picture in place of the screen. The Chief Operations Officer (I) sat near the rear of the 'stalls', with his broadcast officer on his right; in front of them sat the fighter liaison officers in telephone contact with the fighter airfields. Plots on the positions of the raiding force and the defending fighters were flashed on the translucent air situation map from behind.

During the latter part of 1943 Fw 190s began operating against American daylight bomber formations with a new weapon, the Wgr 21 rocket. This improvised weapon comprised a 21-cm spin-stabilized infantry mortar rocket, fired from a simple tube launcher. The weight of the rocket at launch was 111 kg (248 lb), of which 41 kg (90 lb) was warhead. In action both wing-mounted rockets were fired simultaneously, using the B-2 button mounted on the control stick. via Creek

Fitting the time fuse to a Wgr 21, prior to loading. The fuse exploded the missile after a pre-set flight time usually corresponding to a flight time of about 1,000 m. In action, however, the Wgr 21 proved disappointing. It was extremely difficult to judge the range accurately enough so that the rockets detonated within lethal range (about 30 metres/yards) of the target. As a result, the great majority of these missiles exploded harmlessly either short of the bombers or past them.

Armourers lowering a rocket into the launching tube.

Fw 190s of *II./JG 3*, seen carrying a single Wgr 21 launcher under the fuselage. These rockets were in fact fired rearwards, as a parting shot when the fighters overtook the bombers after attacking them with forwards-firing cannon. This use of rockets was not successful, however, and saw little use. via Girbig

CHAPTER 8

JABO PILOT

Initially the Fw 190 was issued only to fighter units but, fast and sturdy aircraft that it was, it was obviously suitable for the fighter-bomber (*Jabo*) role. In August 1942 the IIIrd *Gruppe* of *Zerstörergeschwader 2* was withdrawn from the Eastern Front, and went to Parndorf near Vienna to re-equip. The unit exchanged its Messerschmitt Bf 109 fighter-bombers for Fw 190 A-4s, to become the first *Jabo Gruppe* to equip fully with the new aircraft.

Feldwebel Adolf Dilg served on the unit as a pilot, and he found the Focke Wulf more suitable for the role than its predecessor.

'We found the Fw 190 a great improvement over the Messerschmitt 109E we had been using over Russia. For the *Jabo* role it was better in every respect: it was much faster, it handled better, it was more rugged and easier to maintain in the field and it was much more stable on the ground especially when it had a bomb on board.

'The conversion training lasted about a month then, in September, we moved to Cognac near Bordeaux in France for specialized training in anti-shipping operations. For some time it had been clear that the Allies were building up forces for amphibious assault operations and our unit was one of those in the Luftwaffe assigned to the counter-invasion role. In the mouth of the Gironde an old French destroyer lay aground and against her we

practised low level and dive bombing attacks using 250 and 500 kg [550 and 1,100 lb] cement training bombs. We also received practical training in penetrating the Bordeaux balloon barrage, which proved an exciting business.'

In October 1942 some of the more experienced pilots in the *Gruppe*, Dilg included, were ordered to fly to Merville near Lille. On the final day of the month they, and the similarly equipped *Jabo Staffeln* from JG 2 and JG 26, delivered a thirty aircraft attack on Canterbury, as a reprisal for the increasingly heavy attacks by RAF bombers on German cities. A large force of Fw 190 fighters escorted the fighter-bombers. Dilg recalled:

'On our way in we hugged the surface of the sea, to keep beneath the prying beams of the British radar. The visibility low down was good but above us at 600 m (2,000 ft) there was an almost continuous blanket of cloud: almost ideal weather for our purpose. Keeping out to sea we skirted round the Dover flak defences, then turned due west to cross the coast just to the north of Deal. I think we achieved complete surprise: at the coast a few guns opened up an inaccurate fire against us, but we soon left them behind. Flying at our maximum speed we took only about three minutes to reach Canterbury. We

A close up of the mounting of an SC 250 high explosive bomb (550 lb), on the fuselage rack of an Fw 190.

made for a point just to the north-west of the city, then turned port through a semicircle and ran in to attack. Each Focke Wulf carried a single delayed action 500 kg [1,100 lb] bomb, fused to explode when the last of the attackers had got clear. At the target the defences were fully alert and they opened up at us with everything they had. Particularly disconcerting were the rockets, which left dense trails of smoke as they climbed in front of us on parallel paths; it looked as though they were trying to erect some sort of wire net in the sky to

trap us and I banked steeply to avoid the smoke. Still keeping low, we made our escape along a route similar to that we had used going in. From start to finish, we had been over England less than six minutes.'

In fact there was no 'net'. The smoke trails were made by anti-aircraft rockets fitted with conventional high explosive warheads, fired by a 'Z' battery near Canterbury. The RAF scrambled sixty-three Spitfires and Typhoons to engage the raiders, and there were several combats with the escorts. Two of the latter

Feldwebel Adolf Dilg, pictured in the cockpit of an Fw 190 with his terrier Peter. *Dilg*

were shot down, including one flown by Adolf Galland's brother, Paul, who was killed.

Following the attack on Canterbury, Dilg's *Gruppe* received orders to transfer to Comiso in Sicily.

'We had not been there long when, on 8 November 1942, Allied troops landed in Algeria and Morocco. We received orders to move with utmost possible speed to Tunisia. At last we were to go into action in our designated 'counter-invasion' role. Almost from the moment we arrived at Sidi Ahmed near Bizerta, we were in the thick of the fighting. On 12 November Allied troops captured Bone and the town became their main supply port for the advance into Tunisia. We went into action against shipping off the port but a nasty shock awaited us: the ship put up a veritable wall of flak and in addition we had to face large numbers of enemy fighters.'

It was immediately clear to the pilots that in this theatre *Jabo* operations were going to be far more hazardous than they had been in Russia. On 2 December the *Gruppe* lost its commander, Hauptmann Wilhelm Hachfeld, nicknamed 'Bomben Willi' because of his success as a *Jabo* pilot.

'It was one of those silly accidents well clear of the enemy, which have claimed so many aces. He had just begun his take-off run for an attack on an enemy position when he collided with a Messerschmitt 109 from another airfield which just landed and stopped on the runway. Hachfeld's Focke Wulf nosed over on to its back and caught fire, and he was dead before the rescue team could get him out. From outside our crew room we watched with horror as the drama unfolded, unable to do anything to help.'

The Allies mounted bombing attacks on Sidi Ahmed, though initially with little effect. The defending fighters, Bf 109s from *JG 53* and Fw 109s from *II./JG 2*, dealt severely with several of the early bombing attacks. During an attack on the airfield on 4 December, No. 18 Squadron of the RAF lost all eleven Bisley bombers taking part.

As well as frequent attacks on shipping in the anchorage at Bone, the *Jabo* unit attacked enemy artillery positions, supply dumps and vehicles near the front line. It also flew raids on the Allied forward airfields at Thelepte, Tebessa and Kairouan. At the end of December the *Gruppe* was re-designated as IIIrd of *Schnellkampfgeshwader 10*. The change made no difference to the type of operations flown, and the latter continued as before.

'Most of our attacks were straightforward, though on a few occasions we had to plan attacks on two or three different targets then wait at *Sitzbereitschaft* [cockpit readiness] in our bombed-up aircraft until a last-minute decision on which one we were to go for. This happened if we had to synchronise our attack with one by the army, or if an enemy attack was expected and we were to provide support for our troops when it was launched.'

Gradually the German and Italian forces in Tunisia were squeezed tighter and tighter as the Allies closed in from both the east and the west. In the air the Luftwaffe faced overwhelming enemy forces and its losses began to mount disastrously, such was the pace of operations.

'Throughout my time in North Africa there was no shortage of aircraft, fuel or bombs; but we received very few replacements for the pilots we lost. And the pilots we did get were often straight from training and, lacking experience, did not survive for very long. All too often one would arrive from Sicily in the late afternoon and be killed in action during the next couple of days.

'Things went from bad to worse until at one stage we had no officers left in the *Gruppe* and attacks were led by a Feldwebel. In January the fighter-bomber ace Oberleutnant Fritz Schröter arrived to take command of the *Gruppe*, but by then things had moved beyond the point where individuals could do much to alter the course of events.'

Adolf Dilg's combat flying career came to an abrupt end on 24 January 1943. That day he took off in the fighter role, briefed to provide air cover for a convoy of supply ships making its way from Italy to Tunisia.

'We had just been relieved and I was on my way home when suddenly I saw tracer going past my aircraft; there was a series of bangs, then my Focke Wulf shuddered and burst into flames. We had been

A close up of the bomb fusing selector panel of the Fw 190, mounted beneath the centre of the instrument panel. The electrical bomb fusing system enabled the pilot to select the type of fusing prior to release, thus giving a measure of flexibility when delivering an attack. The simple pointer switch could be set to safe (*Aus*), for diving (*Sturz*) or horizontal (*Wagerecht*) attacks, with delayed fusing (*mit Verzögerung: MV*) or without it (*ohne Verzögerung: OV*). A longer delay fusing was required for low altitude horizontal attacks rather than for dive attacks. Lights above the fusing panel illuminated as each of the bombs was released. VFW-Fokker

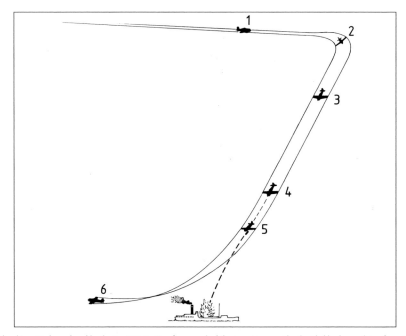

'Rechlin' type dive-bombing attack employed by the Fw 190. 1. Aircraft approached the target to one side, throttled back, as pilot or formation leader assessed wind drift. Altitude about 2,500 m (about 8,000 ft). 2. As target disappeared beneath the wing, the aircraft was banked into the dive. 3. Once in the 50 degree dive the speed built up rapidly, sometimes reaching 800 k.m./h. (500 m.p.h.) at the bomb release point. 4. At an altitude of 1,200 m (about 4,000 ft) the nose was eased up 3 degrees (to ensure that the bomb cleared the propeller) and one second later . . . 5. . . . the bomb was released. Immediately after release the pilot began the pull out, at the same time turning to avoid enemy ground fire. 6. Descending to about 50 m (about 150 ft) the fighter-bomber made its getaway.

"bounced" out of the sun by American Lightnings. I rolled the aircraft on to its back, jettisoned the canopy and baled out. As I was coming down the shock of the encounter began to wear off and I could feel a severe pain in my right forearm. I looked down and my blood ran cold as I caught sight of my flying suit cut to ribbons and my arm bleeding profusely. A cannon shell had passed clean through my arm, shattering the bone.

'By the time I hit the water I had lost the use of my right arm together. With some difficulty I managed to inflate my life-jacket, but my dinghy resisted all attempts to get it to blow up using only one hand. I spent a couple of hours in the water in intense pain then, to my great good fortune, an Italian destroyer hove into view and came almost straight towards me. My distress flares caught the crew's attention and I was picked up. The destroyer took me back to Tunisia, then a few days later I was moved to Italy with other wounded.'

The injuries to Dilg's right arm were so severe that Army doctors decided to amputate it at the elbow. But luckily for him the Luftwaffe got to hear about it, and he was whisked to one of his own service hospitals where the facilities were much better. There doctors removed a piece of bone from his leg and grafted this into his arm to save it. Thereafter he made a rapid recovery, and was able to resume flying later in the year. His subsequent career as an Fw 190 pilot is described in Chapter 20.

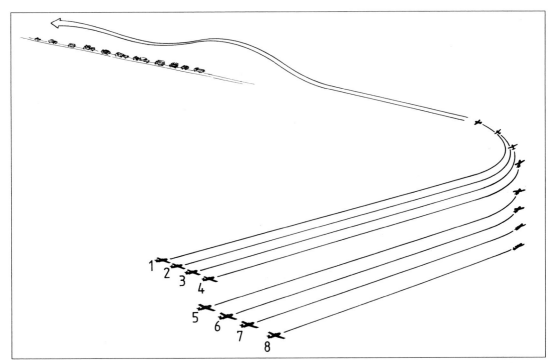

Typical approach for a low altitude attack by Fw 190 fighter-bombers, flying with 80–100 metres/yards between aircraft and 150–200 metres/yards between *Schwärme*. The leader would take the formation to an easily identified point to one side of the target, then turn in for a *Steckrubenwerf* attack with his aircraft following in line astern.

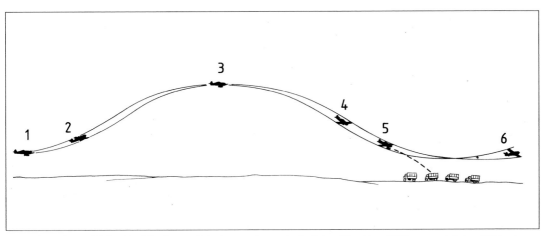

A *Steckrubenwerf* (turnip–lob) low altitude bombing attack. 1. The approach at an altitude of about 50 m (about 150 ft) at a speed of about 500 k.m.h. (310 m.p.h.). 2. About one mile from the target pilot eased up the nose of his aircraft . . . 3. . . . . levelled off at about 300 m (about 1,000 ft) and lined up on the target before going into a shallow descent. 4. He held the target in the centre of his sight. 5. One second before bomb release the nose was eased up 3 degrees, then the bomb was released. 6. Evasive turn and getaway.

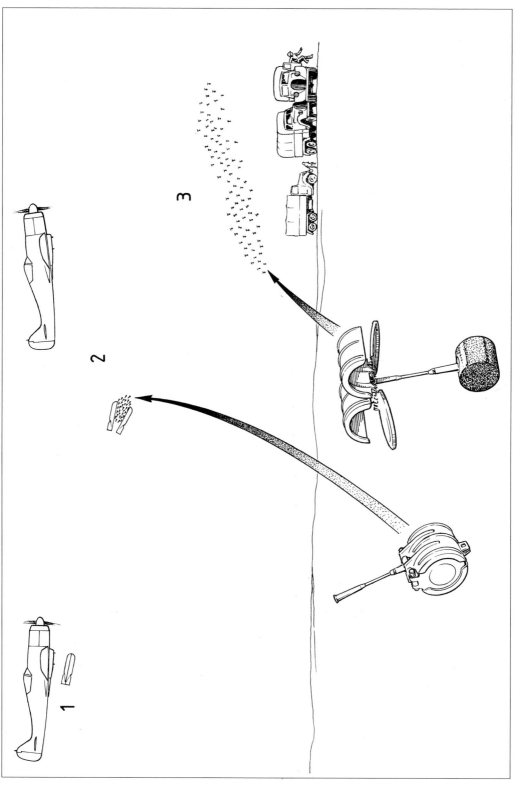

A *Steckrubenwerf* attack with an AB-250 small bomb container. 1. Aircraft releases AB-250 container. 2. When safely clear of the aircraft the container opens longitudinally and 108 SD-2 bomblets fall clear. 3. The SD-2s' wings open and arm the bombs, which then flutter to the ground.

CHAPTER 9

UNITS EQUIPPED WITH FW 190S 17 MAY 1943

LUFTFLOTTE 1 (NORTHERN SECTOR, EASTERN FRONT)

Unit	Total	Serviceable
Jagdgeschwader 54		
Stab	4	4
I. Gruppe	36	30
10. Staffel	9	3[1, 2]

LUFTFLOTTE 2 (ITALY)

Unit	Total	Serviceable
Schlachtgeschwader 2		
II. Gruppe	22	4[3]
Schnellkampfgeschwader 10		
III. Gruppe	20	2

LUFTFLOTTE 3 (FRANCE, BELGIUM)

Unit	Total	Serviceable
Jagdgeschwader 2		
Stab	4	4
I. Gruppe	40	40
II. Gruppe	24	18
III. Gruppe	40	37
Jagdgeschwader 26		
Stab	4	4
II. Gruppe	40	40
III. Gruppe	40	35

A *Staffel* of ground-attack Fw 190s, believed to belong to *SKG 10*, photographed at Deplin-Irena near Warsaw where the unit flew training missions against targets in the nearby bombing range. via Heise

Unit	Total	Serviceable
Jagdgeschwader 54		
11. Staffel	16	9[1]
Schnellkampfgeschwader 10		
Stab	6	6
I. Gruppe	42	42
II. Gruppe	40	38
IV. Gruppe	30	23
Aufklärungsgruppe 123		
4. Staffel	2	2[4]
Nahaufklärungsgruppe 13	31	25

LUFTFLOTTE 4 (SOUTHERN SECTOR, EASTERN FRONT)

Unit	Total	Serviceable
Schlachtgeschwader 1		
Stab	6	6
I. Gruppe	41	32[3]
II. Gruppe	25	17[5]
Schlachtgeschwader 2		
Stab	3	1
I. Gruppe	8	4

LUFTFLOTTE 5 (ARCTIC SECTOR, EASTERN FRONT)

Unit	Total	Serviceable
Jagdgeschwader 5		
Stab	2	2
I. Gruppe	35	23[6]
II. Gruppe	23	20
IV. Gruppe	40	31[6]
14. Staffel	11	7[3]

LUFTFLOTTE 6 (CENTRAL SECTOR, EASTERN FRONT)

Unit	Total	Serviceable
Jagdgeschwader 26		
I. Gruppe	36	30

Unit	Total	Serviceable
Jagdgeschwader 51		
Stab	14	11
I. Gruppe	39	20
III. Gruppe	40	21
IV. Gruppe	28	20

LUFTWAFFENBEFELSHABER MITTE (REICH AIR DEFENCE)

Unit	Total	Serviceable
Jagdgeschwader 1		
Stab	3	1
I. Gruppe	31	27[6]
II. Gruppe	39	31
Jagdgeschwader 11		
I. Gruppe	40	27

NOTES

1. Fighter-bomber unit.
2. Unit forming.
3. Unit also flew Hs 129 ground-attack aircraft.
4. Reconnaissance unit, also operated Bf 109s.
5. Unit also flew Hs 123 and Hs 129 ground-attack aircraft.
6. Unit also flew Bf 109s.

CHAPTER 10

JABOS OVER SICILY AND ITALY

Fw 190A-4 fighter–bomber of *IV. Ergänzungs* (training and replenishment) *Gruppe* of *Schnellkampfgeschwader 10*, pictured at Cognac in the south of France in May 1943. Wenk

Oberfähnrich, later Leutnant, Helmut Wenk of *IV./SKG 10* pictured with his aircraft during training at Cognac. Wenk

Wenk went into action with *III./SKG 10* against the Allied forces in Sicily in July 1943. This photograph shows the unit's operations post, situated under a cork tree just off the airfield at Crotone. From left to right are Ofw Rehwoldt, unidentified (not a pilot), Ofw Rippelsieb (on telephone), Leutnant Klein, Uffz Thrun, unidentified armourer. Wenk

A close shave for Helmut Wenk on 27 July 1943. Due to the ever-present risk of air attack, the fighter-bombers took off from Crotone in rapid succession. On this occasion Wenk was blinded by the dust kicked up by the aircraft in front. His Focke Wulf struck a tree to one side of the airstrip and the aircraft careered away, shedding both wings, the drop-tanks, both undercarriage legs and, fortunately, the bomb. The Focke Wulf finally came to rest halfway down the sloping runway overshoot, bearing a shaken but otherwise uninjured pilot. Wenk

Helmut Wenk taking off from Crotone on 1 August 1943, to attack an Allied munitions dump at Nicosia in Sicily. His aircraft, one of eight engaged in the attack, carried two 300 l (65 Imp. gal.) drop-tanks and one SC 250 (550 lb) bomb. The raiders dive-bombed the dump, setting it on fire, then returned at low altitude. As they flew along the road from Nicosia to Taormina, they strafed supply vehicles. Wenk shot up an armoured vehicle and two lorries, before falling foul of a mobile anti-aircraft gun which scored three hits on his aircraft. He succeeded in reaching Crotone and making a normal landing, but the aircraft never flew again. Two fighter-bombers failed to return from this mission. Wenk

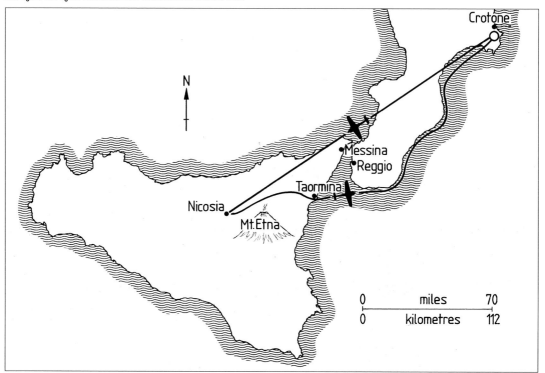

The route flown by the aircraft of *6. Staffel* of *SKG 10* during the attack on Nicosia, Sicily, on 1 August 1943.

Fw 190s of *SKG 10* pictured during the hard fought battles in Italy in the autumn and winter of 1943. Armourers preparing to load an SC 250 (550 lb) bomb on to an aircraft.

With ground crewmen on the wing to guide the pilot to the take-off point, an Fw 190 laden with an SC 500 (1,100 lb) bomb moves out of its dispersal point.

A formation of Fw 190s moving out for an attack.

A dive attack with an SC 500 (1,100 lb) bomb.

The actions round the Allied lodgement area at Anzio in Italy during January and February 1944 were some of the hardest fought of the war. The close-support air command post of *Luftflotte 2* during the Anzio battle, situated in slit trenches overlooking the Allied bridgehead. Present, from left to right, are Oberleutnant Kluge, Generalfeldmarschall Baron Wolfram von Richthofen (cousin of the First World War fighter ace) commanding *Luftflotte 2*, General von Pohl and Oberst Christ.

General view of the command post, with von Richthofen on the far right observing the bridgehead through binoculars. Von Richthofen was the leading German exponent of close-support air operations and frequently took personal command of the air battle.

The view out to sea from von Richthofen's command post, showing Allied shipping burning off the coast following an air attack. Moving with his staff to such close proximity to the enemy was part of his style of leadership. via Rigelsford

CHAPTER 11

FOCKE WULF 190 NIGHT-FIGHTERS

In the summer of 1943 Royal Air Force night bombers successfully used aluminium foil, codenamed 'Window', to jam the German night-fighters' airborne and ground control radars. As a temporary expedient Focke Wulf Fw 190 and Messerschmitt Bf 109 fighters, seeking their prey visually without the use of radar, were pressed into action in the night air defence role under the codename *Wilde Sau* (Wild Boar). VFW-Fokker

The architect of the *Wilde Sau* tactics was Major Hajo Herrmann, pictured here with Hermann Göring during an inspection of pilots. Herrmann

Initially the *Wilde Sau* pilots had to rely on searchlights and fires at the target to illuminate night bombers for them so that they could attack. If there was a layer of cloud over the target the searchlight crews would adopt *Mattscheibe* (ground glass screen) tactics, playing their beams on the base of the clouds so that the light diffused and silhouetted bombers flying above. The success of this method is shown in this photograph, taken looking down on a Lancaster flying over Berlin on the night of 16 December 1943.

Early in 1944 a few Fw 190s were fitted with the *Neptun* radar, to enable them to seek out bombers on their own. This particular aircraft, seen with its pilot Oberleutnant Krause, belonged to the operational trials unit *Nachtjagdgeschwader 10* based at Werneuchen near Berlin and was used on operations during the

summer of 1944. The transmitter aerials were fitted to the rear fuselage, the left/right receiver aerials were fitted above each wing and the above/below receiver aerials were fitted just in front of the cockpit and under the starboard wing respectively. On the nose of the aircraft can be seen the *Wilde Sau* badge, a boar's head.

A close up of the transmitter aerials of *Neptun* radar.

Oberleutnant Krause with his aircraft.

The instrument panel of a radar equipped Fw 190 night-fighter, showing the cathode ray tube for the *Neptun* equipment just below the top coaming.

An alternative aerial scheme for the *Neptun* radar, fitted to some Fw 190s.

CHAPTER 12

ON THE EASTERN FRONT

Fw 190A-3s of *I./JG 51*, the first *Gruppe* on the Eastern Front to re-equip fully with this aircraft, pictured at Velikiye Luki early in 1943. The aircraft in the background to the left is having its engine changed under the most primitive conditions. Romm

An Fw 190A-3 of *II./JG 51*.

Fw 190 fighters of *JG 51* pictured on the central front during the decisive Battle of Kursk in July 1943. via Michulec

No, that is not how you get little Fw 190s. . . . Collision was an ever-present risk on the congested forward airfields in Russia, especially during periods of intensive operations. As it was landing, this Fw 190 of *JG 51* ran over another aircraft of the same unit. via Michulec

Fw 190A-5 of *III./JG 51* pictured after crash-landing near Tschemlysch on the central part of the front in August 1943. via Girbig

CHAPTER 13

THE TABLES ARE TURNED

During the winter of 1943/4 two important new fighter types entered service with the USAAF and the RAF: the North American P-51B Mustang fitted with the Merlin engine, and the Spitfire XIV with the Rolls-Royce Griffon. Before they went into action both aircraft took part in mock combats against a captured Fw 190A, to determine the best tactics to employ against it. The trials revealed that the new Allied fighters possessed sizeable performance advantages over the German fighter. By then the Allied intelligence service knew of the existence of the Fw 190D, the improved variant then in the trials stage. The Fw 190D was expected to go into action at any time (in fact it would not appear until the autumn), and projected performance figures for this variant were given in the report on the P-51B. Excerpts from the trial reports are reproduced below.

FW 190A VERSUS P-51B MUSTANG

MAXIMUM SPEED
The Fw 190 is nearly 50 m.p.h. [80 k.m./h.] slower at all heights, increasing to 70 m.p.h. above 28,000 feet [112 k.m./h. above 8,540 m]. It is anticipated that the new Fw 190D might be slightly faster below 27,000 feet [8,230 m] but slower above that height.

CLIMB
There appears to be little to choose in the maximum rate of climb. It is anticipated that

the Mustang will have a better climb than the new Fw 190D. The Mustang is considerably faster at all heights in a zoom climb.

DIVE
The Mustang can always out-dive the Fw 190.

TURNING CIRCLE
Again, there is not much to choose. The Mustang is slightly better. When evading an enemy aircraft with a steep turn, a pilot will always out-turn the attacking aircraft initially because of the difference in speeds. It is therefore still a worthwhile manoeuvre with the Mustang when attacked.

RATE OF ROLL
Not even a Mustang approaches the Fw 190.

CONCLUSIONS
In the attack, a high speed should be maintained or regained in order to regain the height initiative. A Fw 190 could not evade by diving alone. In defence a steep turn followed by a full throttle dive should increase the range before regaining height and course. Dogfighting is not altogether recommended. Do not attempt to climb away without at least 250 m.p.h. [400 k.m./h.] showing initially. Unfortunately there is not enough information on the new Fw 190D for any positive recommendations to be made.

The North American P-51C Mustang, furthest from camera, possessed several performance advantages over the Fw 190A. This continued with the later P-51D fitted with the bubble canopy (the three aircraft in foreground).

PERFORMANCE OF P-51B CARRYING LONG RANGE TANKS

SPEED

There is a serious loss of speed of 40–50 m.p.h. [65–80 k.m./h.] at all engine settings and heights. It is, however, still faster than the Fw 190 (BMW 801D) above 25,000 ft [7,620 m].

CLIMB

The rate of climb is greatly reduced. It is out-climbed by the Fw 190. The Mustang is still good in a zoom climb (attack), but is still outstripped (defence) if being followed all the way by the Fw 190.

DIVE

So long as the tanks are fairly full, the Mustang still beats the Fw 190 (BMW 801D).

TURNING CIRCLE

The tanks do not make quite so much difference as one might expect. The Mustang can at least turn as tightly as the Fw 190 (BMW 801D) without stalling out.

RATE OF ROLL

General handling and rate of roll are very little affected.

CONCLUSIONS

The performance of the Mustang is greatly reduced when carrying drop-tanks. Half-

The Spitfire XIV, with a similar performance to the P-51C, also enjoyed a measure of superiority over the Fw 190A.

hearted attacks could still be evaded by a steep turn, but determined attacks would be difficult to avoid without losing height. It is still a good attacking aircraft, especially if it has the advantage of height.

FW 190A VERSUS SPITFIRE XIV

MAXIMUM SPEEDS
From 0–5,000 ft [0–1,525 m] and 15,000–20,000 ft [4,573–6,100 m] the Spitfire XIV is only 20 m.p.h. [32 k.m./h.] faster; at all other heights it is up to 60 m.p.h. [97 k.m./h.] faster than the Fw 190A.

MAXIMUM CLIMB
The Spitfire XIV has a considerably greater rate of climb than the Fw 190A at all altitudes.

DIVE
After the initial part of the dive, during which the Fw 190 gains slightly, the Spitfire XIV has a slight advantage.

TURNING CIRCLE
The Spitfire XIV can easily turn inside the Fw 190. Though in the case of a right-hand turn, this difference is not quite so pronounced.

RATE OF ROLL
The Fw 190 is very much better.

CONCLUSIONS
In defence, the Spitfire XIV should use its remarkable maximum climb and turning circle against any enemy aircraft. In the attack it can afford to 'mix it' but should beware of the quick roll and dive. If this manoeuvre is used by an Fw 190 and the Spitfire XIV follows, it will probably not be able to close the range until the Fw 190 has pulled out of its dive.

CHAPTER 14

UNITS EQUIPPED WITH FW 190s 31 MAY 1944

LUFTFLOTTE 1 (NORTHERN SECTOR, EASTERN FRONT)

Unit	Total	Serviceable
Jagdgeschwader 54		
Stab	4	4
I. Gruppe	44	36
II. Gruppe	52	48

LUFTFLOTTE 2 (ITALY)

Unit	Total	Serviceable
Schlachtgeschwader 4		
Stab	3	2
I. Gruppe	14	4
II. Gruppe	27	9

LUFTFLOTTE 3 (FRANCE, BELGIUM)

Unit	Total	Serviceable
Jagdgeschwader 2		
Stab	3	0
I. Gruppe	19	14
III. Gruppe	29	19
Jagdgeschwader 26		
Stab	2	2
I. Gruppe	33	23
II. Gruppe	32	25

Focke Wulf 190 spy planes. These were aircraft from a reconnaissance unit, believed to be the *5th. Staffel* of *Fernaufklärungsgruppe 123* which was based at Le Luc near Toulon in France in the summer of 1944. The fairing over the camera port, which identifies the aircraft as the A4/U4 photographic reconnaissance version, is just visible under the fuselage and the marking.

Unit	Total	Serviceable
Schlachtgeschwader 4		
III. Gruppe	40	36
Schnellkampfgeschwader 10		
I. Gruppe	33	19
Aufklärungsgruppe 123		
5. Staffel	4	2[1]

LUFTFLOTTE 4 (SOUTHERN SECTOR, EASTERN FRONT)

Unit	Total	Serviceable
Schlachtgeschwader 2		
II. Gruppe	42	20
Schlachtgeschwader 10		
Stab	5	2
I. Gruppe	32	16

Unit	Total	Serviceable
II. Gruppe	31	15
III. Gruppe	40	24
Schlachtgeschwader 77		
I. Gruppe	34	32[1]
II. Gruppe	33	21

LUFTFLOTTE 5 (ARCTIC SECTOR, EASTERN FRONT)

Unit	Total	Serviceable
Schlachtgeschwader 5		
I. Gruppe	15	12[2]

LUFTFLOTTE 6 (CENTRAL SECTOR, EASTERN FRONT)

Unit	Total	Serviceable
Jagdgeschwader 51		
Stab	16	16[1]
Schlachtgeschwader 1		
II. Gruppe	12	2[2]
III. Gruppe	42	33

LUFTFLOTTE REICH (REICH AIR DEFENCE)

Unit	Total	Serviceable
Jagdgeschwader 1		
Stab	2	2
I. Gruppe	43	15
II. Gruppe	42	20
Jagdgeschwader 3		
IV. (Sturm) Gruppe	54	1[4]
Jagdgeschwader 11		
I. Gruppe	28	20
III. Gruppe	28	11
10. Staffel	10	7[1]
Jagdgeschwader 54		
III. Gruppe	23	8

A split pair of RB 12.5 cameras, mounted in the rear fuselage of an Fw 190. These short focal length cameras were used for low altitude reconnaissance. For high altitude operations, longer focal length cameras were necessary. VFW-Fokker

Unit	Total	Serviceable
Jagdgeschwader 300		
Stab	2	1
II. Gruppe	32	23
Nachtjagdgruppe 10	4	2[3]
Schlachtgeschwader 3		
III. Gruppe	34	31[4]

NOTES

1. Unit also operated Bf 109s.
2. Unit also operated Ju 87s.
3. Night-fighting trials unit, operated several other types.
4. Unit in the process of forming or reforming.

CHAPTER 15

NO PLACE FOR A BEGINNER

'In no other profession are the penalties for employing untrained personnel so appalling or so irrevocable as in the military.'

General Douglas MacArthur

During the early months of 1944, Feldwebel Fritz Buchholz flew the twin-engined Messerschmitt Me 410 bomber-destroyer with *II./ZG 26*, based at Königsberg/Oder. As US escort fighters ranged progressively deeper into German territory, however, the heavy fighters suffered such severe losses that they had to cease operations. In July Buchholz's unit was redesignated IInd *Gruppe* of *Jagdgeschwader 6* and it began converting to the Fw 190 fighter. The pilots received only the sketchiest training in flying their new mounts, before they were ordered into action.

'On 3 August 1944 I made my first flight in the Fw 190. I found the aircraft pleasant to fly, though after the excellent ground visibility of the Me 410 the massive motor cowling of the Focke Wulf was disconcertingly restrictive. Flying against the heavy bombers in the Me 410 had been rather like driving one truck against another; fighter-versus-fighter combat in a Fw 190 was something quite different. This might not have been so bad, had there been sufficient time for us to assimilate our new role. But this was not the case. The battle round the allied bridgeheads in Normandy was entering its most critical

phase and we were to go into action as soon as possible. On 18 August, just over two weeks later and with 10 hours 54 minutes flying time in the Fw 190, I received orders to depart with the *Gruppe* for France on the following day.'

Flying in easy stages, the *Gruppe* took four days to move from Königsberg to its forward operational base at Herpy near Reims with the forty-odd Fw 190A-8s. At that time the Allied air superiority was such that the permanent Luftwaffe bases in France were being bombed regularly. Operational units were forced to use improvised airstrips in the surrounding countryside; the move had been planned before the invasion, and fields were surveyed and stocked with the necessary fuel and ammunition.

'Our airstrip at Herpy was nothing more than a piece of flat cow pasture surrounded by trees in which our aircraft could be hidden; nearby was our tented accommodation. The Allied fighter-bombers seemed to be everywhere and our survival depended on the strictest attention to camouflage. As part of this we even had a herd of cows which were moved on to

Fritz Buchholz's Fw 190, No. 21, pictured at Königsburg/Oder during the rapid conversion of *II./JG 6* to the type. Note the full-sized B-17 painted on the hangar doors, to assist pilots in judging the range when making a head-on attack on a heavy bomber. Buchholz

the airfield when no flying was in progress. As well as giving the place a rustic look, these performed the valuable task of obliterating the tracks made on the grass by the aircraft. Such attention to detail paid off and there were no attacks on Herpy while I was there.'

On the day following his arrival at Herpy, 23 August, Buchholz made three flights in order to get to know the local area. On the 24th he made another. On none of these flights did he come into contact with the enemy aircraft, though some members of his *Gruppe* did. Compared with the previous permanent airfield deep inside Germany, operations from the ill-equipped forward airfield were rather more difficult: 'Although our small pasture was excellent for the point of view of camouflage, the confined space did make it difficult for the unit to get airborne rapidly. During our first day there two aircraft collided during take-off, probably because one of them had run into the turbulent slipstream from the pair that had taken-off immediately ahead.'

By the time the *Gruppe* was ready to go into action from Herpy, the Battle of France was already lost. The German retreat from Normandy was in its closing stages, with troops streaming eastward across the Seine. II./JG 6 was sent into action to cover the moves.

'On the third day after our arrival in France, 25 August, we took off for our first full-scale operation: a sweep by the entire *Gruppe* as far as the Seine or as directed by our ground controller when we were airborne. Led by our commander, Hauptmann Elstermann, the forty-odd Fw 190s took off shortly after noon. So sketchy had our training been that this was the first occasion on which II./JG 6 had flown together as a *Gruppe*. My *Staffel*, the 7th, was to fly as top-cover and so took off first; we orbited the field while the others got airborne, then the large formation climbed away to the west with our *Staffel* about 6,000 ft above the other two.'

Soon after leaving Herpy the *Gruppe* received new orders. Enemy fighter-bombers were attacking the airfield at Chastres near St Quentin, and the Focke Wulfs were to engage these. Elstermann turned the *Gruppe* on to a northerly heading and shortly afterwards Buchholz caught sight of some aircraft a few miles away to the north, below the level of his *Staffel* but above the main part of the formation.

'I called the *Gruppe* commander: "*Achtung, Fragezeichen von rechts*"

[Attention, unidentified aircraft to the right]. He acknowledged my call and identified the aircraft as American P-38 Lightnings. With the sun on our backs we went after them and as we got closer I counted about twelve. Elstermann gave the order "*Zusatzbehülter weg!*" and the drop-tanks tumbled away from the aircraft.'

'My *Staffel* commander, Oberleutnant Paffrath, took us down to attack. I took my *Schwarm* to follow him in a tight turn, but suddenly my Focke Wulf gave a shudder. The wing dropped and I found myself spinning helplessly into the mêlée below. I had to take the standard spin recovery action, pushing the stick forwards and applying opposite rudder, with the dogfight going on all around me. It was utter chaos, with Focke Wulfs chasing Lightnings chasing Focke Wulfs. I recovered from my spin and fired a burst at one Lightning, only to have to break away when another Lightning curved round and opened fire at me.'

Then Buchholz discovered the cause of his spin: his drop-tank was still in place, and now it resisted all his efforts to release it. Almost full of fuel, it weighed about 250 kg (about 550 lb). No wonder his aircraft could not turn as tightly as the others that had dropped their tanks!

The twelve P-38s that they had attacked belonged to the 394th Squadron of the 367th Fighter Group. Heavily outnumbered, the twin-engined fighters began to take losses. There were frantic radio calls for assistance, and the other two squadrons in the US Group broke off their attacks on other airfields in the area and sped to the scene. Buchholz continued:

'Our initial attack hit the Americans hard and I saw some Lightnings go down. We

Feldwebel Fritz Buchholz, thrown into action with II./JG 6 after his hasty conversion from the Me 410 to the Fw 190, discovered the hard way that an air battle was no place to learn the brutal art of dogfighting. Buchholz

might have been new to the business of dogfighting, but with the advantage of the sun and numbers we held the initiative. The surviving American fighters twisted and turned, trying to avoid our repeated attacks.

'Then, suddenly, there seemed to be Lightnings diving on us from all directions: now it was our turn to become the hunted. Obviously far more experienced than we were in fighter-versus-fighter combat, the American pilots who had just arrived on the scene cruised overhead selecting their victims, then dived down in pairs to pick them off before zooming back to altitude. We were being chopped up by experts and I watched Focke Wulf after Focke Wulf go down.

'I climbed and tried to rejoin the fight, moving in to cover the tail of a Focke Wulf without any protection. But as I got there a pair of Lightnings came down after us; he went into a tight turn and as I tried to follow him I found myself spinning out of control again. I repeated this unnerving experience a couple more times before deciding to give up; my meagre experience in handling the Fw 190 was insufficient for this situation and the middle of a dogfight was no place to learn. I was doing nothing to help my comrades and if I stayed around much longer I would almost certainly make an easy victim for one of the Lightnings. I broke away and dived to low altitude, making good my escape. I landed back at Herpy, taxied to my dispersal point, shut down the engine and clambered out; my flying suit was wringing wet with sweat.'

In ones and twos the surviving Focke Wulfs landed at Herpy, some bearing the scars of battle. As the afternoon wore on it became clear that the *Gruppe* had experienced a disaster. Sixteen of its aircraft had been destroyed, fourteen pilots were killed or missing and three more were wounded. Among the missing was the commander of the *8th Staffel*, Leutnant Rudi Dassow, a highly successful Me 410 pilot with twenty-two kills to his credit. Buchholz's *Staffel* commander, Oberleutnant Paffrath, was wounded. During the engagement the American Group lost seven Lightnings, six of them from the 394th Squadron attacked initially.

The scale of the losses on 25 August came as a great shock to Buchholz and his comrades. 'With so many aircraft destroyed and damaged, our fighting strength had been reduced by about a half during a single engagement. We were indeed learning the lessons of combat the hard way. Yet we had little time to mourn our comrades: the battle was continuing and the retreating German ground troops were taking a terrible beating from the Allied aircraft.'

On the following day, 26 August, the surviving Focke Wulfs of II./JG 6 were again ordered to patrol the River Seine to cover the German withdrawal. Buchholz led his *Schwarm* to the briefed patrol area near Rouen.

'Soon after our arrival in the battle area, we were "bounced" from out of the sun by Mustangs. I never even saw the aircraft that hit me. All I heard was a loud bang and the next thing I knew my aircraft was tumbling out of the sky with part of the tail shot away. I blew off the canopy and struggled to get clear of the spinning aircraft, but my right foot became wedged under the instrument panel. After what seemed an age I managed to wrench it away, though I left my flying boot behind and my foot collided with the tailplane as I was falling clear. My parachute opened normally and I landed on the west bank of the Seine near Duclair. A rearguard unit of the SS picked me up and took me to their field dressing station, where one of their doctors removed a metal splinter from my left foot and bound it up. During the night I was taken across the river on board an army ferry.'

The retreating army unit carried Buchholz 140 miles, to the Luftwaffe airfield at Juvincourt near Paris. Allied spearhead units were nearing the area and everyone was getting ready to leave. 'Every serviceable aircraft had already left, and army engineers had placed demolition charges ready to blow up the runway and taxi tracks. Somebody suggested that I might like to fly out a partially serviceable Fw 190, which would otherwise have to be blown up. I jumped at the chance. I thought that no flight in an aircraft could possibly be worse than the journey I had just made by road.'

There were a few small problems, however. At Juvincourt all stores had either been moved out or destroyed. Buchholz had no flying helmet, parachute or map. The Focke Wulf's guns had no ammunition and there was fuel for only about 40 minutes' flying. A folded blanket in the seat well filled the space normally occupied by the parachute. With his foot bandaged, the German pilot was lifted into the cockpit. Few flights have begun less auspiciously, and that point was drummed home to Buchholz when he was strapped in.

'As I was about to start the engine, an engineering officer appeared and said that the aircraft was unfit to fly. He would accept no responsibility for it in its present condition: quite apart from several uncleared faults, it had recently been involved in a very heavy landing which had strained the tail and possibly the undercarriage as well. I told him that under the circumstances I was happy to accept responsibility for the aircraft. Freed of the possibility of future recriminations, he agreed to let me take it.'

Buchholz took off, aiming to get to the Luftwaffe airfield at Florennes near Namur in Belgium. That was about 80 miles away as the crow flies, but lacking a map he could not take the most direct route.

'I decided to follow the line of the Aisne river and canal to Sedan, then the Meuse river which flowed close to Florennes. Soon after take-off the first problem manifested itself: the undercarriage refused to retract. With the gear down the limiting speed of the Fw 190 was 160 m.p.h.; if I was spotted by enemy fighters, I would be easy meat. Even so, I reasoned, I was far better off in an aircraft going at 160 m.p.h. than a car moving at 30 m.p.h.. There could be no thought to returning to Juvincourt, having got this far. I kept low to avoid trouble.

'After about twenty minutes' flying, however, things began to go really wrong. I suddenly noticed that the needle of the oil temperature gauge was rising past the danger mark. This was bad news: the rear cylinders of the BMW 801 always ran hot and if there was any failure in their lubrication the engine was liable to seize. Now I really was in a fix. I had no parachute so I could not bale out, and if I crash-landed with the undercarriage extended, and the ground was not hard enough, the aircraft was liable to nose over on to its back. As the oil temperature rose still higher it became clear that I had better choose a field soon, and get the Focke Wulf down while the motor still had some life in it. If the engine failed suddenly I would have no choice where I landed.'

Buchholz picked out a reasonably large flat field, and turned towards it. He decided to land in a hard side-slip to port, hoping this would wipe off the undercarriage and the aircraft would then slide to a halt on its belly. He had no notion of the amount of thought Kurt Tank and his team had put into designing a really strong undercarriage for the fighter.

'The undercarriage proved stronger than I had expected. It held. The port wing took the main force of the impact and buckled. The aircraft then swing round, the motor struck the ground so violently that it broke right away, the fuselage then rolled over and finally come to rest upside-down. Bruised all over and covered in blood, I managed to fight my way out of the cockpit.'

'As I stood up beside the wrecked Focke Wulf I saw men running towards me. My first horrified thought was "Oh God, partisans!" If they caught me like this they would probably slit my throat from ear to ear. Fortunately for me, however, they turned out to be simple farmers. They took pity on my miserable condition and helped me to their village where a German army vehicle later picked me up.'

Buchholz spent the next six weeks in hospital recovering from his various wounds, then he rejoined II./JG 6 which by then was based at Üdenbach near Bonn. 'When I arrived there were only three or four survivors out of the forty or so half-trained pilots that had set out with me to go to France in August; the remainder were either dead, wounded or in enemy prison camps. Shortly afterwards I was sent to a training unit, to help convert ex-bomber pilots on to the Fw 190.'

Fritz Buchholz's combat career as a single-engined fighter pilot had lasted exactly two missions: during the first he had had a hard fight merely to stay alive, during the second he was shot down and wounded. So far as he was aware, his presence failed to cause the slightest inconvenience to the enemy. In the summer of 1944, the skies over France were no place for a beginner.

The hard-fought battle at midday on 25 August 1944 took place between *II./JG 6* and the US 367th Fighter Group. The American Group, equipped with the P-38 Lightning, comprised the 392nd, 393rd and 394th Squadrons. Twelve P-38s of the 394th Squadron had been strafing the airfield at Clastres when they were 'bounced' by Fw 190s of *II./JG 6*. Answering the call for help from the 394th, the twenty-one Lightnings from the other two Squadrons abandoned their attacks on nearby airfields and went to their comrades' assistance. During the ensuing action *II./JG 6* lost sixteen aircraft. The 376th Group lost seven P-38s, six from the 394th Squadron. Pictured here is Captain Lawrence E. Blumer, who led the 393rd Squadron during the action and was credited with five of the Fw 190s destroyed. USAF

CHAPTER 16

IF NECESSARY, BY RAMMING

'If your bayonet breaks, strike with the stock; if the stock gives way, hit with your fists; if your fists are hurt, bite with your teeth.'

General Mikhail Dragomirov, *Notes for Soldiers*, 1890

During the spring of 1944 the fighter units defending the German homeland faced a discomforting problem. To engage the

A line up of Fw 190 A-8/R8s belonging to a *Sturmgruppe*. Note the barrel of the 30-mm cannon protruding from the wing just to one side of the undercarriage leg.

American four-engined bombers with any prospect of success, their aircraft needed to carry batteries of heavy cannon or rockets. Yet, weighed down with such weapons, the defending fighters fell as easy prey when they were engaged by the American escorts.

As a solution to this problem, two new types of fighter *Gruppe* were formed. The *Sturmgruppen* were equipped with heavily armed and armoured versions of the Fw 190, and these were to engage the bombers. The *Begleitgruppen*, units equipped with lightly armed fighters, were to hold off the American escorts while the *Sturmgruppen* delivered their attacks.

Leutnant Walther Hagenah flew Bf 109s on the Eastern Front with *I./JG 3*, before his unit was pulled back to assist with the defence of the homeland late in 1943.

'During our initial home defence operations we experimented with several different forms of attack against the four-engined bombers: from directly behind, diving from above, diving from above and pulling up to attack from underneath, even from directly in front. Between December 1943 and May 1944 my personal score amounted to five heavy bombers, four

B-17s and one B-24. But although my own and the other air defence *Gruppen* were having some success, it was clear that far more of the heavy bombers would have to be knocked down if the Americans were to cease their devastating attacks on our homeland. Moreover, with the appearance of their long range escort fighters deep over Germany, things were getting more difficult with each month that passed.'

In July 1944 Hagenah accepted an invitation to join IV. *(Sturm) Gruppe* of *JG 3*, commanded by Hauptmann Wilhelm Moritz. The unit, based at Ilesheim, was the first of three *Sturmgruppen* then being formed.

The *Sturmgruppe* differed from a normal air defence fighter unit in three fundamental respects: in the dedication of the volunteer pilots who served in it, in the aircraft it operated and in the tactics it was to employ. Every pilot who volunteered to join a *Sturmgruppe* had to sign the following affidavit: 'I . . . do solemnly undertake that on each occasion on which I make contact with an enemy four-engined bomber I shall press home my attack to the shortest range and will, if my firing pass is not successful, destroy the enemy aircraft by ramming.'

Any volunteer who signed the affidavit, and failed to carry out its conditions, would be liable to face a court-martial charged with cowardice in the face of the enemy. Yet no man was forced to sign the affidavit, and there were no recriminations against those who refused to do so. These men simply joined the ranks of the *Sturmgruppen*.

The second point of difference between a *Sturmgruppe* and normal fighter unit was that the former operated the Fw 190A-8 R8 version, with additional armour and a much heavier armament. The R8 sub-type carried nearly twice as much armour as the basic Fw 190A-8. The armour round the nose ring

Leutnant Walther Hagenah flew the heavily armoured *Sturmbock* version of the Fw 190A-8 during the summer of 1944. Hagenah

was thicker, as was that behind the pilot's head. There was additional armour around the base of the windscreen, round the ammunition boxes for the heavy cannon mounted in the outer wing, and down each side of the cockpit. Large slabs of toughened glass were fitted on each side of the canopy, with other pieces on each side of the windscreen. Like the normal A-8, the R8 carried a pair of 13-mm machine-guns above the engine and two 20-mm cannon in the wing roots, all synchronized to fire through the propeller disk. But in place of the 20-mm weapons in the outer wing positions there were two powerful MK108 30-mm cannon. The R8, nicknamed the *Sturmbock* (battering ram), was about 200 kg (440 lb) heavier than the basic Fw 190A-8. With the extra weight, the fighter was slower in the climb and rather less crisp on the controls than a standard aircraft.

With their more dedicated pilots and specialized aircraft, the *Sturmgruppen* were to employ tactics that would be extremely hazardous for a normal fighter unit. Walther Hagenah explained:

'In the past we had flown in open tactical formations, attacked the bombers in twos and fours, and it was up to individual *Rotte* [pair of aircraft] and *Schwarm* [four aircraft] leaders to decide when to open fire and when to break away. In the *Sturmgruppe*, however, it was quite different. We flew in a close arrowhead formation by *Staffeln*, with the *Staffel* leader in the front and the other aircraft in echelon on either side of him with two or three yards between each aircraft. Succeeding *Staffeln* followed close behind, each slightly lower than the one in front. When the *Sturmgruppe* leader had positioned his force behind a *Pulk* of bombers he would allocate aircraft to engage different parts of the enemy formation. For example the leading *Staffel* might receive orders to engage the high squadron of bombers, the next might take on the middle squadron and the third *Staffel* might take on the low squadron of bombers. The form of the attack was therefore much more formal than anything I had used before.'

Once a *Sturmstaffel* was in position about 1,000 yards behind 'its' squadron of bombers, the *Staffel* leader ordered his aircraft into line abreast. Then, maintaining close formation, the heavily armoured Fw 190s advanced on the bombers.

'Our tactics were governed by the performance of our wing-mounted 30-mm cannon. Although the hexogen high-explosive ammunition fired by this weapon was devastatingly effective, the gun's relatively low muzzle velocity meant that its accuracy fell off rapidly with range. And since we carried only 55 rounds per gun, sufficient for about five seconds' firing, we could not afford to waste ammunition in wild shooting from long range. To be sure of bringing down a bomber it was essential that we held our fire until we were right up close against the bombers. We were to advance like Frederick the Great's infantrymen, holding our fire until we could see "the whites of the enemy's eyes".

'During the advance each man picked a bomber and closed in on it. As our formation moved forwards the American bombers would, of course, let fly at us with everything they had. I can remember the sky being almost alive with tracer. With strict orders to withhold our fire until the leader opened up, we could only grit our teeth and press on ahead. In fact, however, with the extra armour, surprisingly few of our aircraft were knocked down by the bombers' return fire. Like the armoured knights of the Middle Ages, we were well protected. A *Staffel* might lose one or two aircraft during the advance, but the rest continued relentlessly on.'

The Focke Wulfs continued their advance on the bombers until they were about 100 yards behind their prey. Then the leader opened fire, followed by the rest of the *Sturmbock* aircraft.

'From such a range we could hardly miss. As the 30-mm explosive rounds struck home, we could see the structure of the

A close up of the cockpit of a *Sturmbock*, officially designated the Fw 190A-8/R8. Note the canopy side-panels of thick laminated glass, also the layer of steel armour mounted on the outside of the fuselage to protect the pilot from rounds coming from the side.

enemy bombers literally falling apart in front of us. On average, three hits with 30-mm ammunition would be sufficient to knock down a four-engined bomber. The shortest burst was usually sufficient to achieve that. On four occasions during *Sturmgruppe* actions in the summer of 1944 I got into position behind an American bomber, and on each of these I shot one down: a B-24 on 7 July, B-17s on the 18th and 20th, and a further B-24 on 3 August.'

If a *Sturmgruppe* got into a firing position behind an American bomber formation, it could do a great deal of damage. Getting

there was not easy, however. Sometimes the German fighter controllers failed to bring about an interception. The greatest problems of all were caused by the American escort fighters.

'Flying in our special Fw 190s, in close formations which were quite unsuitable for fighter-versus-fighter combat, we were extremely vulnerable to attack. To enable us to get through to the bombers, therefore, we had our own escort of two fighter *Gruppen*. My *Sturmgruppe* had the I. and II. *Gruppen* of *Jagdgeschwader 300*, with Messerschmitt Bf 109Gs, allocated for this purpose. The formation

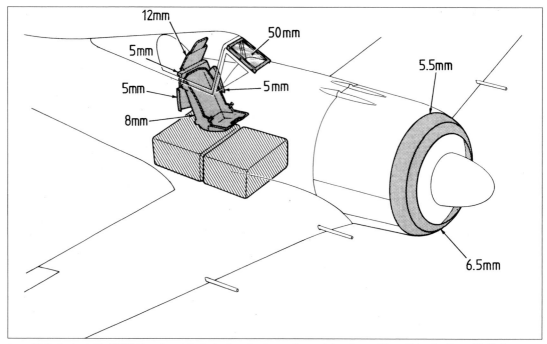

Armour fitted to the standard Fw 190A-8. The main protection for the pilot and engine came from steel plates 5 mm to 12 mm thick, with a 50-mm slab of bullet resistant glass protecting the pilot's head from fire from ahead. The self-sealing fuel tanks under the pilot's seat provided him with useful protection from fire from below.

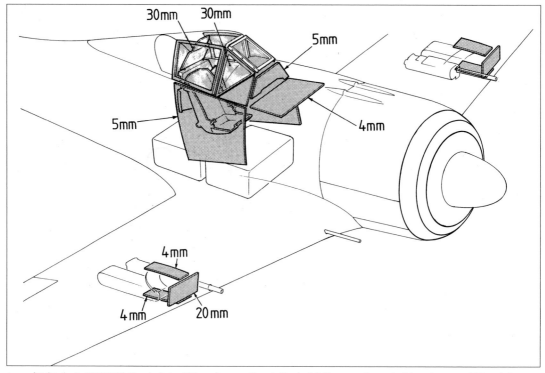

Armour fitted to the Fw 190A-8/R8 *Sturmbock, in addition to* that normally carried by the A-8. The upper side panels of the cockpit were of 30-mm bullet resistant glass, the lower panels of 5-mm steel plate. Steel plates protected the magazines for the 30-mm high explosive cannon shells.

Sturmbock aircraft of *IV./JG 3*, with Hauptmann Wilhelm Moritz in the lead, about to take off from Schongau in the summer of 1944.

Sturmgruppe pilots from Hagenah's *Staffel 10./JG 3*, pictured in August 1944. From left to right are, unidentified, Uffz Kröber, Uffz Volz, Oberleutnant Hans Weik (Hagenah's predecessor in command of the unit, with his arm in plaster after being wounded in action), Leutnant Hagenah, FW Schäfer, Uffz Vohl, Uffz Dreddla and Uffz Hentrich. On the far right is Hauptfeldwebel Maxeiner, the unit's senior ground crewman. The photograph was taken at Burggen, a few miles from Schongau airfield, where the men were billeted. Hagenah

comprising the *Sturmgruppe* with its two escorting *Gruppen* was known as the *Gefechtsverband* [battle formation] and numbered about ninety aircraft.

'Usually our escorts were able to ward off the American fighters. But on occasions when we did come under fighter attack, our position was difficult. Not only were our aircraft heavy, but few *Sturmgruppe* pilots had much experience in dogfighting. So, in general, we tried to hold close formation and press on towards the bombers even if a few enemy fighters managed to break through our escort to attack us. We thought it better to lose some aircraft and have a chance to shoot down the bombers, rather than split our

Feldwebel Hans Schäfer, wearing his leather flying jacket with the 'Whites of the Eyes' insignia worn by some *Sturmgruppe* pilots. Schäfer was credited with twenty-seven victories, including eight against four-engined bombers. Schäfer

formation and lose a few aircraft but shoot down no bombers at all. It was a difficult decision to make, and on occasions it led to heavy losses. On some occasions the rear *Staffel* of the *Sturmgruppe* was ordered to turn round and engage enemy fighters that had broken through the escort, but this was the exception rather than the rule. The worst time for the enemy fighters to hit us was when the *Gefechtsverband* was forming up. If they caught us then, they could throw the whole thing into confusion and the operation had to be abandoned.'

In the event there were very few occasions when *Sturmgruppe* pilots found it necessary to ram an enemy bomber. Walther Hagenah never did so and he never saw anyone else do it.

'The paper we had signed indicated an absolute moral commitment to bring down enemy four-engined bombers, if necessary by ramming. But if we held our formation, ran the gauntlet of the bombers' defensive fire and reached a firing position 100 yards behind a bomber, with our powerful cannon it was a relatively simple matter to get a kill. There were a few occasions when people reached a firing position and found, for example, that their weapons had jammed. Then they opened their throttles, pulled up a little, dived down and rammed. By and large, however, our weapons were very reliable and that was rarely necessary.

'We received no detailed instructions from our High Command on how best to ram the enemy bombers though the matter was, of course, the subject of several discussions in our crewroom. Of

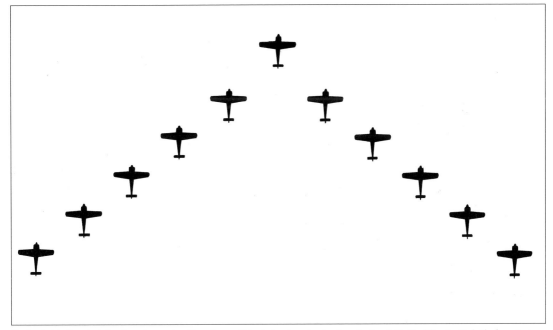

The *Breitkeil* (wide-wedge) close formation employed by a *Sturmstaffel* as it closed on a bomber formation from behind to deliver its attack. The formation is drawn to scale.

the pilots who made ramming attacks, about a half escaped without serious injury. One who did not was Obergefreiter Heinz Papenburg of another *Sturmgruppe*, II./JG 4, who rammed and destroyed a B-24 on 27 August 1944. He struck the bomber going really fast and severed one of his wings in the process. As he baled out of his tumbling Focke Wulf he hit the tailplane and smashed both of his legs. He descended by parachute and had to take the shock of the landing on his broken legs, which must have been terrible for him.'

In September 1944 Walther Hagenah left the *Sturmgruppe* to attend a fighter leaders' course. During the final weeks of the war he flew Me 262 jet fighters. Looking back at his time flying with the *Sturmgruppe*, what were his impressions?

'Thinking about it all now, sitting in the comfort of an armchair, it is easy to overemphasize the personal danger of being a *Sturmgruppe* pilot. But it should be remembered that we were in the front line in wartime, where conditions of absolute safety did not exist. Certainly the risks to us were no greater than, say, those accepted by an infantryman charging an enemy position.

'As members of a *Sturmgruppe* we knew that we were a tough unit, something special, and morale was high. There were no shirkers; people like that simply did not accept the harsh conditions of membership. The enemy was system-atically destroying our homeland and we were determined to hit back hard. I am proud to have been numbered among the *Sturmgruppe* pilots. If the conditions were ever repeated, I would do the same thing again.'

The Rheinmetall-Borsig MK108 30-mm cannon seen with one of its high explosive shells. The low muzzle velocity of this weapon dictated the short range engagement tactics employed by the *Sturmgruppen*; the cannon fired rounds weighing 330 g (11½ oz) with a muzzle velocity of 540 m/sec (1,750 ft per sec) at a rate of 660 per minute.

This B-17 Fortress of the 457th Bomb Group was lucky to get home to its base at Glatton in eastern England, after being shot up by German fighters. The damage to the port wing is consistent with hits from one or two 30-mm explosive rounds. On average, three such hits were sufficient to bring down a heavy bomber. USAF

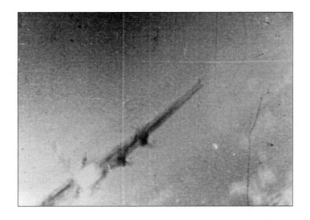

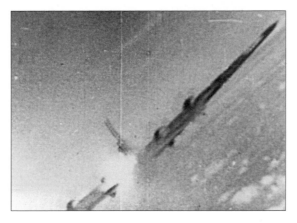

One that did not get home. Stills from the cine film taken by Uffz Maximowitz of *IV. (Sturm)/JG 3*, as he delivered an attack from short range on a B-17 of the 447th Bomb Group on 29 April 1944.

CHAPTER 17

THE LUCK OF THE GAME

Unteroffizier Ernst Schröder was another pilot who volunteered to join a *Sturmgruppe*. During his time with *II. (Sturm)/JG 300* he accounted for seven enemy aircraft, of which two were heavy bombers. In this vivid first-person account he describes his part in the operation on 17 December 1944. The reader will notice some differences between the tactics his unit employed, and those described in the previous section. This is because the methods used by the *Sturmgruppen* had evolved over time, and some tactical points were left to the discretion of the *Gruppe* commander.

Lobnitz bei Bitterfeld, 10.00 hours, 17 December 1944. It is about an hour since the four *Staffeln* of II. (Sturm) *Gruppe* [of *Jagdgeschwader 300*] have been brought to readiness. The aircraft have been moved from their dispersal pens in the nearby wood, on to the airfield. On arrival the ground crews check the security of each aircraft's 300 litre [66 Imp. gal.] drop-tank, in case the journey over the rough taxi-track has shaken it loose. Then a refueller runs down the lines of aircraft, topping up each in turn. The thirty-odd Fw 190 *Sturmbock* aircraft, those ready for action, have been lined up on the airfield by *Schwarme*. The pilots, wearing leather flying suits and yellow life-jackets, stand around chatting close to their machines.

While this is going on I, an Unteroffizier and *Schwarm* leader, wait almost alone at the 5th *Staffel* dispersal area. My aircraft has developed a fault and although the ground crew are working feverishly on it, it is not yet airworthy. I hang around impatiently: any minute now we might get the order to scramble.

Suddenly there is a bang and a red signal flare rises from the operations building: cockpit readiness! My comrades climb into their aircraft and strap in, assisted by their mechanics. The stillness returns. The sun shines through the trees at the dispersal pens, now empty except for my aircraft with its panels removed and four or five 'grease monkeys' poking round inside.

Suddenly the loudspeakers round the airfield boom out: 'Achtung Achtung, Unteroffizier Schröder to the *Gruppe Stab* dispersal area, aircraft "Blue 13" is ready!' I grab my parachute and gallop the couple of hundred metres to where the aircraft stands. The Focke Wulf, a blue number '13' painted on its side, used to belong to Oberstleutnant Dahl who was our previous *Geschwader* commander.

Just as I am about to get into the aircraft a green flare soars into the sky: scramble! The stillness round the airfield is shattered as BMW 801 engines burst into life and aircraft begin moving towards the take-off point. Hastily I buckle on my parachute and

An Fw 190A-8 of *II.(Sturm)/JG 300* coming in to land at Löbnitz, towards the end of 1944. Schröder

clamber into the cockpit as the mechanics help me to strap in. Damn! The position of the armoured seat and the rudder pedals has been adjusted to suit Oberstleutnant Dahl, a man who is somewhat shorter than I am. I now find myself cooped up uncomfortably with my knees bent back almost double. And there is no time to do anything about it: already the three 'young hares' of my *Schwarm* are moving up to the take-off point. With a roar my motor starts (it has already been warmed up). I taxi out of the dispersal and on to the airfield, just as the last of the other aircraft are getting airborne. I line myself up on the runway and slam open the throttle; thrust along by 1,800 horsepower, the machine accelerates rapidly after the others.

The formation leader on this occasion, Leutnant Bretschneider who commands the *5th Staffel*, climbs away making a wide sweep to the left so that everyone can form up as rapidly as possible. I straggle behind, gaining slowly despite the fact that I have cut the corner. The formation is at about 1,500 m [5,000 ft] before I catch up with the rear. Then I have to pick my way through the 'crowd', searching for the leaderless *Schwarm*. Fortunately I find the other three quite quickly and am in position by the time

Unteroffizier Ernst Schröder flew with *5./JG 300*. He used this aircraft, Red 19, on most of his operations between August and the end of November 1944. On 27 November the machine was hit during a fight with Mustangs, and it was wrecked during the subsequent belly landing at Köthen. Schröder

they give details of the whereabouts of the American bomber formations, which have come from Italy and are passing over southern Austria heading northwards.

Picking its way between the towering pillars of clouds, the formation climbs higher. As we pass 4,000 m [13,000 ft] each man clamps on his oxygen mask. In spite of Bretschneider's skilful leadership in steering the formation between the larger clouds, he is unable to prevent our passing through the occasional small one. Then, flying in close proximity to so many other aircraft is an unpleasant experience.

Once we are above cloud, at last I have a little time to look round the aircraft I am flying. It is the most heavily armed Focke Wulf on our unit, with two 30-mm cannon, two 20-mm cannon and two 13-mm machine-guns (most aircraft in our *Gruppe* lack the 13-mm guns). With all of these weapons and the additional armour, it is a typical *Sturmbock*: an unwieldy 'dungheap' weighing more than 5 tons and quite unsuitable for dogfighting. That and my cramped sitting position will make it difficult to carry out the task assigned to me: with my *Schwarm* I am to provide a final line of protection for the *Strumgruppe* from attacks by enemy escort fighters. My usual aircraft, now sitting uselessly on the ground, is a normal Fw 190A-8 without extra guns or armour.

The formation continues its climb into the clear blue winter sky, with a few course corrections ordered from the ground. From time to time, at around 5,500 m [18,000 ft], short condensation trails form behind our aircraft but they disappear almost immediately. For some time the radio has been silent; perhaps we are off on another *Gammeleinsatz* [wild goose chase]. Our feelings are mixed, alternating between fear and hope.

we reach Wittenberg on the Elbe: this is the assembly point for the whole *Geschwader* and is marked by coloured smoke puffs from signal rounds fired from the ground by the flak people. From the right and below other fighters approach: the Messerschmitt Bf 109s of our escorting *Gruppen*.

After a couple of orbits at 2,500 m [8,000 ft] the *Geschwader* formation is complete: some thirty Fw 190s of the *Sturmgruppe* escorted by fifty or sixty Messerschmitts. Flying just underneath the cloud base, we receive orders from the Fighter Divisional headquarters at Döberitz near Berlin to climb on a south-easterly course. Over the radio

We begin to receive further reports from the ground: the incoming bomber formation is on a northerly heading *Hanni 80* [altitude of enemy aircraft 8,000 metres, 26,000 ft]. Far beneath us the Silesian landscape unrolls. Beyond our formation there is nothing else to be seen in the sky: no other condensation trails, no glittering reflections from other aircraft. It is all deceptively peaceful.

Within a few seconds, the picture changes completely. A series of crackling orders and course changes come through our earphones, each one more urgent and impatient than the last. Finally the controller announces: 'You have the *dicke Autos* [fat cars: heavy bombers] ahead! You should be able to see them now!' We all stare into the sky: nothing.

One thing is clear, however: this is going to be no *Gammeleinsatz*. In each aircraft the pilot checks that his gunsight is switched on and his armament safety switches are to 'fire'. Suddenly we hear Bretschneider's urgent call on the radio: '*Victor, Victor von Specht Anton. Ich sehe dicke Autos! Wir machen Pauke-Pauke!*' [Loose translation: 'Roger, Roger, this is Woodpecker leader. I see the bandits! Tally-ho!'] With my four aircraft I have to protect the *Gruppe* from enemy fighters coming in from the left, so I position my *Schwarm* about 90 m [300 ft] above the main body of the formation to get a better overall view. Then I catch sight of the glittering reflections of the sun on the uncamouflaged American bombers: they are obliquely to the left of us and at the same altitude, about 7,600 m [25,000 ft]. Still a long way away, the stately enemy formation crosses in front of us from left to right. I carefully search the sky for enemy escorts, but I can make out only three or four condensation trails above the bombers.

On the order, each Fw 190 lets go of its drop-tank and they tumble earthwards. Then Bretschneider swings our formation a little to

Leutnant Klaus Bretschneider, the commander of *5./JG 300*, led the *Sturmgruppe* during the action on 17 December 1944. Bretschneider had a remarkable career, starting his score as a *Wilde Sau* night-fighter pilot when he accounted for fourteen enemy bombers. He then transferred to *Strumgruppe* operations and destroyed several more bombers, including one by ramming on 10 October 1944. A week after the action described in this section, on Christmas Eve 1944, Bretschneider was killed during a fight with P-51 Mustangs. Schröder

the left, to put us on a reciprocal heading to the enemy bombers. The leading enemy 'combat box' passes by with a wide margin: it comprises fifteen or twenty B-24 Liberators with red-painted tails, an imposing sight. Just before the second 'combat box' comes past, our formation begins a moderately tight right-hand turn to slot into position between it and the third. With my *Schwarm* I continue a few seconds longer straight ahead, keeping a sharp lookout to the front and above for

Unteroffizier Matthaus Erhardt, Bretschneider's wingman. He was seriously wounded in action on 14 January 1945. Schröder

Leutnant Norbert Graziadei succeeded Klaus Bretschneider as commander of 5./JG 300.

enemy fighters; still there are none. Then I curve round after the rest of our formation. The *Sturmgruppe* is now directly in front of me, about 45 m [150 ft] below; I have a grandstand view of the attack as it unfolds. Behind me is the third 'combat box'; but it is too far away for the bombers' front guns to present any danger and in any case the bombers themselves are flying much slower than we are. We are now flying exactly in the stream of enemy bombers, rapidly overhauling the second 'combat box'. Above us I can make out a few P-38 fighters, but it seems that we have taken them by surprise and they do not come down to attack. Perhaps they are calling up reinforcements.

In front of me the drama unfolds rapidly. The bombers open up a furious defensive fire, filling the sky with tracer. It seems that none of us can avoid being hit. We at the rear of the formation weave a little, to make things difficult for the American gunners. The entire

Sturmgruppe moves in at full throttle, to close the range on the enemy bombers as rapidly as possible. At 300 m the main body of the Fw 190s opens up with their 20-mm and 30-mm cannon, the murderous trains of high explosive shells streaking out towards the Liberators. Within seconds two of the giant aircraft have exploded into great fireballs, while several others have caught fire and are falling out of the formation. In strong contrast to the strict radio discipline that had reigned previously, the ether becomes a babble of voices: '*Horrido!*' ('I've got him!'), 'He's on fire!', 'All assemble to the right and above', 'I'm hit, bailing out' and so on.

With my *Schwarm* I now close in on the shattered enemy formation. I make a quick check to see that the sky behind us is clear of enemy fighters, then I lead my Focke Wulfs in to attack. I select a Liberator and at 300 m I press the firing button. Damn! Nothing happens! The bomber gets closer and closer,

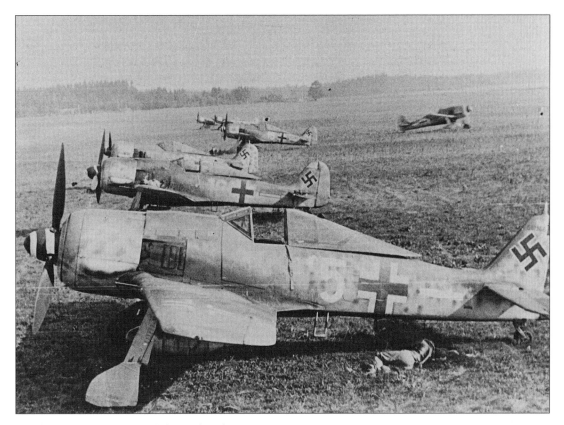

Pilots of *II.(Sturm)./JG 300* waiting beside their aircraft at Löbnitz.

50 – 40 – 30 m, an ideal firing position! Swearing like a deranged man I press and re-press the electrical circuit breakers for the guns and the firing button, but still I cannot get them to fire. On either side of me my *Schwarm* comrades fire like mad and score hit after hit on their targets. At the last moment I push down the nose of my Focke Wulf, then pull up with the rest of the *Gruppe* to the right and above the bombers. Looking around, the sky is like a chaotic circus: whirling and fluttering pieces of aircraft, an entire wing falling complete with engines and propellers still turning, several parachutes,

and some of our aircraft battling with the few P-38 escort fighters that have reached us.

Enraged and frustrated, I continue with my efforts to discover the reason for the failure of my armament. But all is in vain, I cannot get off a single round. Now I am no use to anyone so, infuriated with the aircraft, I push down the nose to dive away steeply and break off the action.

I land my Focke Wulf at Liegnitz in Silesia at 12.30 hours, having been airborne for almost exactly two hours. There my aircraft is quickly refuelled and I take off again at 14.10 hours and land back at Löbnitz twenty minutes later.

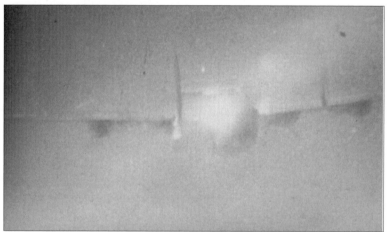

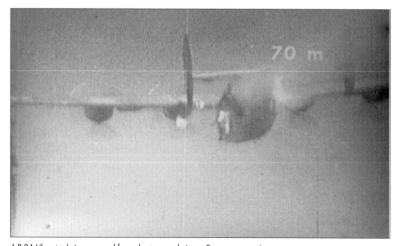

A B-24 Liberator being engaged from short range during a *Sturmgruppe* action.

Ground running an Fw 190A-8/R8 at Löbnitz. Beside the port wing tip is Leutnant Spenst, commander of *8./JG 300*. Schröder

I taxi the machine back to the *Gruppe Stab* dispersal area where it had come from. No sooner have I shut down the engine then I begin to tear a strip off the ground crewmen for giving me an aircraft whose guns do not work. One of them reaches into the cockpit, however, and quietly points to an extra gun safety switch fitted to this particular Fw 190: it is still set to 'safe'. The system is slightly different from that fitted in any of our other aircraft and I could not have known about it.

Earlier in the year, under the rules of membership in a *Sturmgruppe*, I should have

been expected to bring down an American bomber by ramming if my guns had failed to do so. But in December 1944 the shortage of trained fighter pilots in the Luftwaffe is so grave that this suicidal form of attack is no longer required. When the facts of the matter are made known to my commander I receive no reproof.

Looking back on the incident, I am pleased for the sake of ten American airmen on board that Liberator that my guns did not work. Had they done so the bomber would almost certainly have been torn to pieces and they would have had little chance of survival.

On 11 August 1944, near Gutersloh, an Fw 190 carried out the first airborne firing of the Rhurstahl X-4 air-to-air guided missile. Powered by a liquid fuel rocket motor, the X-4 was steered in flight by command signals transmitted down thin wires unreeled from the weapon as it sped towards the target. With a maximum range of about 3,000 metres, the X-4 weighed 60 kg (132 lb) at launch. The 20 kg (44 lb) high explosive warhead was fitted with acoustic proximity, impact and self-destroying fuses. The acoustic proximity fuse, of doubtful effectivness, was to be triggered by the engine noises from the heavy bomber. Had the war continued, the X-4 would almost certainly have been the first air-to-air guided missile used in action.

The trial installation of the X-4 joystick control unit fitted in the cockpit of an Fw 190.

CHAPTER 18

EASTERN FRONT *JABO*

In May 1944 Leutnant Werner Gail joined *III./Schlachtgeschwader 3* at Pardubitz, as the unit was in the process of converting from the Junkers Ju 87 dive-bomber to the Fw 190F. The conversion process was cut short, however, as a grave crisis erupted far to the east: 'In June 1944 my unit was suddenly ordered to the Eastern Front. The massive steamroller of the Russian summer offensive had just begun its move westwards. Almost immediately the enemy broke through in several places and their armoured units were thrusting into our undefended rear areas. As rapidly as possible we moved to Dünaburg in Lithuania, then east to Idriza in Russia.'

As Gail quickly discovered, the air operations on the Eastern Front were characterized by the large ground forces employed by the enemy and the fluid nature of the battle front.

'During this period the ground situation was so fluid that we had to start each day with an armed reconnaissance: two or three *Schwarme* were sent to patrol different parts of the area assigned to our *Gruppe*, to see if the enemy had moved and if so where. Since we soon came to know our area well and we knew where the enemy had been the night before, we had a good idea where to start looking for him the following morning. Also, whenever enemy armoured units had broken through, they would advance through open country which made the task of finding them much easier.'

Once the morning reconnaissance had returned and the pilots had delivered their reports on the latest positions of enemy troops, the *Gruppe* was allocated the targets for the day in order of importance.

'Our task was to do all we could to delay the thrusts, to give German ground forces time to improvise defensive positions to stop the rush. Wherever there was a hole in the front, it was our job to try to plug it.

'Our Focke Wulfs were armed with two 13-mm machine-guns and two 20-mm cannon, which we used for strafing attacks. The bombs we used during these operations were mainly 250 and 500 kg [550 and 1,100 lb] and also SD-2, SD-4 and SD-10 bomblets carried in large numbers in containers. When we found enemy units moving forwards unopposed, as a matter of policy we concentrated our attacks on the soft-skinned supply vehicles; these were relatively easy to knock out with machine-gun and cannon fire and we knew that without frequent replenishment of fuel the tanks spearheading the advance would not get far. If the enemy armoured units were actually in contact with our ground forces, however, then the tanks themselves were our main target.'

The normal force employed during these attacks was the four aircraft *Schwarm*, though against the larger enemy troop concentrations sometimes as many as twelve aircraft would be sent. Usually the fighter-bombers approached their targets at altitudes of around 1,800 m [6,000 ft], above the effective reach of the enemy light flak. However, if there was a layer of cloud, the aircraft would remain beneath it in order to maintain contact with the ground.

'Against the enemy tanks and armoured vehicles we usually made skip bombing attacks, running in at speeds of around 485 k.m./h. [300 m.p.h.] at between 4 and 10 m [15 and 30 ft] above the ground and releasing the bomb just as the tank disappeared beneath our engine cowling. The 250 kg bombs used during these attacks would either skip off the ground and into the tank, or else smash straight into the tank; the bombs were fused with a one second delay, to give us time to get clear before they went off. It was a very accurate form of attack and we used it often against the tanks we caught in open country. Once we had released our bombs, we would use up our cannon and machine-gun ammunition against suitable targets round about.'

During the initial phase of the Russian offensive Gail's *Gruppe* sometimes flew as many as seven or eight sorties per day. Since the enemy troops were never far from the airfield, these sorties lasted on average only about half an hour. The Red Air Force concentrated its attention against the German rear areas, and the German fighter-bombers were allowed to conduct their operations with little interference. 'Only rarely did we come into contact with Russian fighters. I personally saw them on only two occasions

and on neither did we lose an aircraft. Even so, the general view of the more experienced people on the Eastern Front was that in the summer of 1944 the Russian fighters were much more active than they had been during previous years.'

The sheath of armour protecting the Fw 190F pilot from rounds coming from ahead, below and from the sides, proved very effective against small calibre rounds. Nothing could stop a hit from a heavier calibre anti-aircraft weapon, however. 'Sometimes we caught Russian units that had outrun their flak cover and then we could do a lot of damage and suffer hardly any losses ourselves. But if the enemy units had proper flak cover, our losses were sometimes heavy.'

Throughout July, August, September and October 1944 the German troops, and Gail's *Gruppe*, were pushed steadily westwards. Army Group North, to which the fighter-bomber unit was assigned, was squeezed into the Courland Peninsula in Latvia and ordered to hold its ground. The main Soviet advance continued on its way moving west and leaving the troops in the pocket isolated.

'Initially the pace of operations was very high. But from the end of August the general fuel shortage throughout the Luftwaffe began to make itself felt and we had to reduce consumption. Towards the end, it sometimes happened that before missions our aircraft had to be towed by oxen from their dispersals to the take-off point; and after landing we had to shut down our engines immediately and await the towing crew. When the Russians were actually attacking the pocket, however, the High Command was initially able to scrape some fuel together and while the battles lasted we often flew as many as five sorties a day.'

Fw 190F fighter-bombers of *Schlachtgeschwader 2*, photographed at Sopoc/Puszta in Hungary in January 1945 (*and opposite*). Obert

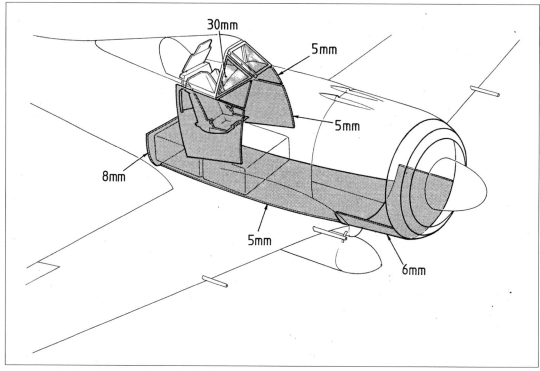

Fw 190F ground-attack aircraft, showing the armour fitted to this version in addition to that normally carried by the Fw 190A-8 fighter.

After a time even the emergency stocks of fuel were almost exhausted. The fighter-bombers flew less and less, until in the early months of 1945 Gail's unit flew scarcely at all. He had one further noteworthy fight to make before the surrender, however.

'My Gruppe stayed in the Courland pocket until the very end. Only on the day of the armistice, 8 May 1945, did we receive permission to fly our aircraft out. That afternoon I took off from Nikas with four ground crewmen squeezed into my Focke Wulf. For the passengers the flight of almost 600 miles to Schleswig Holstein was long and uncomfortable; but neither so long nor so uncomfortable as was the Russian captivity for those left behind.'

FOCKE WULF FW 190F-8

Type: Single-seat fighter-bomber

Armament: Two Mauser MG 151 20-mm cannon with 250 r.p.g., one mounted in each wing root and synchronized to fire through the airscrew. Two Rheinmetall MG 131 13-mm machine-guns with 475 r.p.g., mounted on top of the engine cowling and synchronized to fire through the airscrew. War load of up to 500 kg (1,100 lb) of bombs, cluster bombs or rockets carried on racks fitted under the wings or fuselage.

Power Plant: BMW 801D-2 air-cooled 14-cylinder radial engine rated at 1,700 h.p. for take-off, driving a VDM three-bladed constant speed airscrew. Fuel capacity: 115 Imp. gal. (525 l) in two self-sealing tanks under the cockpit. Provision for one 66 Imp. gal. (300 l) drop-tank on the fuselage rack.

Weights: (empty, equipped) 7,328 lb (3,323 kg); (operational, take-off) 9,700 lb (4,400 kg).

Dimensions: Span, 34 ft 5½ in (10.51 m); length, 28 ft 10½ in (8.8 m); wing area, 197 sq ft (18.3 m²).

Performance (clean): Max speed 342 m.p.h. (550 k.m./h.) at sea level, 394 m.p.h. (634 k.m./h.) at 18,045 ft (5,500 m); initial rate of climb, 2,110 ft/min (10.71 m/sec). Range 466 miles (750 km).

Leutnant Werner Gail, of *III./SG 3*, with his Fw 190F fighter-bomber. Gail

Ground crewman climbing out of the fuselage hatch of an Fw 190. During rapid deployments and evacuation operations, passengers were often carried in the rear fuselage.

An Fw 190 fitted with an experimental installation for the remarkable SG 113 Förstersonde anti-tank weapon. The streamlined fairing in each wing housed the barrels for two of these weapons mounted vertically. As the aircraft flew low over the enemy vehicle, a magnetic sensor triggered the system to ripple-fire the four barrels in rapid succession. As each 77-mm armour-piercing shell was fired downwards, a counterweight was fired simultaneously upwards from the opposite end of the barrel to balance the recoil forces. The weapon performed successfully during its test firings early in 1945, but so far as is known it was never used in action.

CHAPTER 19

DELIVERING THE FOCKE WULFS

In his earlier account, Adolf Dilg described the fighter-bomber operations he had flown over England and Tunisia. That part of his service in the Luftwaffe ended early in 1943 when he was wounded in action. Although his left arm was saved, it had been weakened and he could not return to operational flying.

The move did not end his flying career, however. By the mid-war period the Luftwaffe was desperately short of trained pilots. Those who were semi-fit were sent to second-line flying tasks, to release fit pilots who could be sent to frontline units. Yet, as Dilg recounts, during the closing months of the war a second-line pilot's life was not altogether lacking in excitement.

Brand new Fw 190s off the production line, awaiting test flights and delivery to the Luftwaffe.

'Following my medical downgrading in October 1943, after my repaired right arm was found to be too weak for operational flying, I spent a short period flying communications aircraft. Then I was sent to the Arado factory at Warnemünde near Rostock, for duties as a test and delivery pilot. By the spring of 1944 the factory was turning out Focke Wulf 190s at the rate of about 180 per month. These all had to be test flown, then ferried to units all over the place: to Russia, to the north of Norway, to France and to Italy.

'During the delivery flights we flew with loaded guns; with Allied long range fighters becoming more and more active over our territory, the likelihood of having to face attack while in transit increased with each month that passed. Some of our ferry pilots were shot down but I was lucky. The only time I met enemy fighters, four Mustangs near Nuremburg, an Me 262 jet fighter chanced on the scene and the American fighters broke off the chase.'

By this stage of the war the German armed forces were critically short of manpower. Factory workers were being drafted into the army almost regardless of the military importance of their work. At the aircraft plants their places were taken by half-trained women, and half-starved forced labourers from the occupied territories. The reliability of the latter was, to say the least, questionable. Adolf Dilg and his colleagues encountered several instances where new aircraft coming off the production line had been sabotaged.

'Sometimes we would find bits of metal swarf in electrical junction boxes, or sand in oil systems. On two or three occasions brand new Focke Wulfs took off for their maiden flights and as they lifted off the ground one of the wheels fell off; the pin holding the wheel retaining ring had "accidentally" come adrift.

'Once, when I was delivering an aircraft, the engine suddenly burst into flames. I baled out and the aircraft crashed into a marshy area where the water rapidly extinguished the flames. When the wreckage was examined, it was found that somebody had jammed a couple of pyrotechnic flares between cylinders Nos 7 and 9, the two at the bottom of the rear row which became hottest when the engine was running. During the delivery flight the cylinders had duly heated up, "cooked-off" the flares, and up went the engine.

'Every time we had such an incident the Gestapo would make a lot of fuss, but although they would take the odd scapegoat the problem of sabotage was one we had to live with.'

During 1944 the steady contraction of the area under German occupation was brought home to those delivering the replacement aircraft, as their flights became progressively shorter. From the autumn of that year, the majority of aircraft were delivered direct, without the need for a refuelling stop en route.

'When the end came, even we delivery pilots became caught up in the rush to evacuate German women and children from areas threatened by the Russian advance. In the middle of March 1945 we received orders to evacuate all aircraft from Kolberg [now Kolobrzeg in Poland], just before it fell. I flew out a Focke Wulf 190 with the armour plate behind my seat removed. In its place there crouched a twelve-year-old girl. The radio had been

An Fw 190F fighter-bomber, fitted with dust filters on each side of the engine cowling, starting up in a cloud of smoke at Tutow. Dilg

Ground running an Fw 190F prior to a delivery flight. The '75' painted in black on the cowling was a factory marking. Dilg

Delivery flight of an Fw 190 destined for *JG 5* from Anklam to Bardufoss in Norway. The accompanying aircraft was a Bf 109. Dilg

removed from the rear fuselage and there huddled her mother, who had first to remove all metal objects from her clothing so as not to interfere with the master compass beside her. Another of the ferry pilots, Gefreiter Herzmann, flew an Fw 190 out of Kolberg with a young child on

each knee and their mother in the rear fuselage.'

Evacuation transport: this must have been the purpose furthest from the minds of Kurt Tank and his team when they designed the aircraft seven years earlier.

The fighter ace Hauptmann Walter Nowotny (in uniform) pictured with Focke Wulf test pilots. From left to right, Hans Kampmeier, Werner Fink, Rolf Mondry and Alfred Motsch. Nowotny was killed in action in November 1944 in an Me 262 jet fighter. At the time of his death his confirmed victory total stood at 258, most of them achieved while flying Fw 190s with *JG 54* on the Eastern Front. Sander

Damaged aircraft outside the burning factory at Tutow, where Fw 190s were assembled, following an air attack. This plant came under attack from American heavy bombers on 20 February, 9 April, and 13 and 19 May 1944. Dilg

The Fw 190 A-8/U1 was a two-seat conversion trainer of the famous fighter, built in small numbers. Note the bulged canopy over the rear cockpit on some aircraft, to give a slightly better view forwards from the rear seat (*and opposite*).

CHAPTER 20

ENTER THE LONG-NOSED DORA

'If necessity is the mother of invention, warfare is the mother of development.'

Sir Christopher Foxley-Norris

In the summer of 1944 the first examples of the Focke Wulf 190 Dora began to roll off the production lines. At first glance this fighter, like its predecessor, appeared to be a radial-engined machine. But in fact it was powered by the Junkers Jumo 213, a liquid-cooled in-line engine. The annular radiator was positioned in front of the engine, making for a particularly neat installation. One of those who flew the new variant was Oberleutnant Oskar-Walter Romm: 'I first saw the Dora-9 in December 1944, at Stargard near Stettin. The aircraft had just been delivered from the Focke Wulf works at Marienburg near Danzig in East Prussia. At that time I belonged to the *IV. (Sturmgruppe) of Jagdgeschwader 3 'Udet'*, which operated the Fw 190A-8 and was engaged in the air defence of the Reich.'

In January 1945 Romm assumed command of the *15. Staffel*, and in the following month he took command of *IV. Gruppe*. Operating from Stargard, Romm's unit was tasked with escorting aircraft mounting bombing and strafing attacks on Soviet forces advancing on Berlin and Stettin.

'I was very keen to get hold of the Fw 190D-9, because I could see that before long we should be engaged in a war on two fronts against on the one side the Russians and on the other the British and American fighters and bombers. For such fighting I considered the D-9 to be the ideal aircraft. I succeeded in getting one full *Staffel* equipped with this version, as well as my *Gruppe Stab* with four of these aircraft plus one reserve. To get some of the aircraft we had to rescue them from airfields about to be overrun by the enemy, in spite of the risks involved.

'All our Dora-9s were fitted with the Jumo 213A engine which, with water methanol injection, developed 2,240 horsepower. As an air superiority and interceptor fighter the Fw 190D-9 handled better than the Fw 190A; it was faster and had a superior rate of climb. During dogfights at altitudes of between about 3,000 and 7,500 m [10,000 and 24,000 ft], usual when engaging the Russians, I found that I could pull the Fw 190D into a tight turn and still retain my speed advantage. In the Fw 190A I had flown previously, during dogfights I had often to reduce to minimum flying speed in the turn. In the descent the Dora-9 picked up speed much more rapidly than the Fw 190A; in the dive it could leave the

Focke Wulf 190D-9s of *Stab IV./JG 3* at Prenzlau in March 1945. The aircraft are at readiness, with parachutes on their tails. Romm

Russian Yak-3 and Yak-9 fighters standing.'

Romm's final combat mission took place on 24 April 1945 when, south of Stettin, he attacked a formation of Russian 'Sturmovik' ground-attack aircraft with his wingman.

'I selected full emergency power and with our superior speed we went right through the Russian fighter escort without difficulty. I was just about to open fire on one of the Ilyushins when my cooling gills suddenly opened automatically and the oil and coolant temperature gauges showed that the engine was overheating. Either my engine had been hit by enemy fire or it

had suffered a failure. I broke off the action by rolling on to my back and pulling away in a steep dive. Russian fighters endeavouring to follow were soon left behind and they abandoned the chase.

'The combat had taken place over an area where the Russians had just broken through. So I flew for as long as possible on my dying engine, heading towards the south west and the German front line. From the exhausts a thin line of smoke trailed behind the aircraft, becoming gradually thicker and darker before thinning again with a lot of sparks. As the last of the lubricating oil burned away between the aluminium pistons and the steel cylinder block, the engine burst into flames.

'By now I was over friendly territory. I wanted to bale out, but there was not enough height. The engine stopped altogether and what followed was halfway between a crash and a crash-landing. I suffered a fractured skull, facial injuries, brain concussion and other less serious injuries. Later that day I was picked up by men of my unit and taken to the Luftwaffe hospital at Wismar. My part in the war was over.'

Oberleutnant Oskar-Walter Romm flew Fw 190D-9s with *IV./JG 3* during the final stages of the war. When he was invalided out of action on 24 April 1945 his victory score stood at ninety-two. Romm

Romm's personal Fw 190D-9, bearing the chevrons of a *Gruppe* commander in front of the fuselage marking. Romm

Romm's reserve Fw 190D-9, on the ground at Prenzlau. The aircraft bore the chevron of a *Gruppe* adjutant on the fuselage, although Romm's adjutant had not qualified as a fighter pilot and never flew it. Romm

An Fw 190D-9 taking off for a ground-attack mission during the closing stages of the war, with an AB500 small bomb container under the fuselage. This aircraft is believed to belong to *II./JG 26*, which operated from Nordhorn at this time. via Girbig

FOCKE WULF FW 190D-9

Type: Single-seat general purpose day-fighter.

Armament: Two Mauser MG 151 20-mm cannon with 250 r.p.g., one mounted in each wing root and synchronized to fire through the airscrew. Two Rheinmetall MG 131 13-mm machine-guns with 475 r.p.g., mounted on top of the engine cowling and synchronized to fire through the airscrew.

Power Plant: One Jumo 213A-1 liquid-cooled 12-cylinder in-line engine rated at 1,776 h.p. for take-off, with MW-50 water methanol injection to give increased power for limited periods at low and medium altitude. Drove a VDM three-bladed constant speed airscrew. Fuel capacity: 115 Imp. gal. (525 l) in two self-sealing tanks under the cockpit. Provision for one 66 Imp. gal. (300 l) drop-tank under the fuselage rack.

Weights: (empty, equipped) 7,695 lb (3,490 kg); (max. take-off) 10,672 lb (4,840 kg).

Dimensions: Span, 34 ft 5½ in (10.51 m); length, 33 ft 5¼ in (10.192 m); wing area 197 sq ft (18.3 m²).

Performance: Max speed, 426 m.p.h. (686 k.m./h.) at 21,650 ft (6,600 m); time of climb to 6,560 ft (2,000 m), 2 mins 1 sec, to 19,680 ft (6,000 m), 7 min 6 secs; service ceiling, 43,300 ft (13,200 m).

CHAPTER 21

AN INTRODUCTION TO 'BEETHOVEN'

'You will usually find that the enemy has three courses of action open to him. And of these, he will adopt the fourth.'

Helmut von Moltke

During 1944 Luftwaffe staff officers completed work on an ambitious plan to strike at the Russian armament industry. The factories in the Moscow and Gorky areas depended for their power on twelve steam and hydroelectric generating stations situated in those regions. If these power stations could be put out of action, it would cause a massive drop in military production.

The weapon chosen for the attack was the novel 'Beethoven' device (also known as the *Mistel*: mistletoe). This comprised an Fw 190 fighter rigidly mounted on struts above a Junkers Ju 88 bomber (an earlier version used a Bf 109 mounted on a Ju 88). The bomber's crew compartment was removed and in its place was fitted a 3,500 kg [7,800 lb] high explosive warhead. The pilot sat in the cockpit of the fighter and throughout the flight he controlled the combination from there. The movements of the fighter's stick and rudder pedals were relayed electrically to the automatic pilot in the Ju 88, which moved the bomber's control surfaces in synchronism with those of the fighter – it was probably the world's first fly-by-wire aircraft control system to be used in action. When the pilot reached the target area he aligned the combination on the target, engaged the

autopilot, then fired the explosive bolts to separate the fighter from the bomber. The latter continued straight ahead and, hopefully, flew into the target where the huge warhead detonated.

Two bomber units, *Kampfgeschwader 30* and *200*, were chosen to carry out the operation. As the former unit began preparations for the attack, Oberstleutnant Berhard Jope was appointed its commander. Jope, one of the outstanding German bomber pilots, had started the war flying Focke Wulf 200s against Allied shipping in the Atlantic. In 1943 he commanded *III./KG 100* flying with Dornier Do 217s, which carried out some spectacular attacks on Allied warships using the Fritz-X guided bomb.

When Jope took up his appointment, the unit was at Prague/Ruzyne. He arrived to find it in a state of transition. *KG 30* possessed no bombers and the pilots, like those of other disbanded bomber units, were being re-trained to fly fighters. The other crewmen had been posted away. Jope expected that any day he and his pilots would be sent to a home defence fighter unit.

'I moved to my *Geschwader* headquarters airfield at Ruzyne near Prague. A few days

A fully operational 'Beethoven'. An Fw 190 mounted on an explosive laden Junkers 88, seen in its camouflaged blast pen at Oranienburg early in 1945. This was almost certainly one of the aircraft intended for the abortive *Eisenhammer* operation, with the large 1200 l (264 Imp. gal.) drop-tank mounted under the fighter. Schliephake

after my arrival, I received orders to make myself and my senior officers available for a top-secret briefing from officers of Göring's personal staff. The officers duly arrived and the main part of the briefing was given by a civilian professor from the intelligence department. He began by telling us about "Beethoven", the codename of one of the 'secret weapons' from which great things were expected.'

After describing the new weapon the civilian, Professor Steinmann, outlined a major operation, then in an advanced state of preparation, in which it was to be used.

'Codenamed *Eisenhammer* [iron hammer], it involved a large scale coordinated air strike on the important power stations feeding Russian industry in the Moscow and Gorky regions. These targets, comparatively small and well-protected by concrete, were almost invulnerable to attack by ordinary bombs. If we could deliver one or two "Beethoven" warheads on each, however, it would be a different matter. If the equipment in the power stations could be destroyed or damaged, the Russians would certainly find it difficult to effect repairs; many of the turbines and much of the generating

A training version of the 'Beethoven', with the original Ju 88 cockpit left in place and occupied by a second pilot who landed the combination at the end of the flight.

equipment had originally come from Germany, before the war.'

For this specialized type of operation, the "Beethoven" system offered several advantages over a conventional bomber. It delivered a warhead far more powerful than that carried in any conventional bomb, and the method had a good chance of scoring hits on a large target. More than a hundred "Beethoven" combinations were being made ready for the operation. The attackers were to take off from the airfields at Oranienburg, Parchim, Rechlin-Lärz, Marienehe and Peenemünde in East Prussia. The most distant targets were nearly 1,600 km (1,000 miles) away to the east.

The unwieldy combinations were to penetrate the Soviet defences at night, when the latter were at their least effective. Several Heinkel He 111s, Junkers Ju 88s and Ju 290s were to serve as pathfinders, dropping coloured flares to mark the route. The combinations were to deliver their attack at first light.

For the operation each Fw 190 would carry a large 1,200 l (264 Imp. gal.) drop-tank. But during the flight to the target its engine would run on fuel drawn from the Ju 88's tanks. Thus, at the time of separation, the fighter's own tanks would be almost full. To save weight, each Focke Wulf had its armament removed. Once it was free of the encumbering Ju 88, its high speed gave it a good chance of avoiding interception during the return flight in daylight. A few fighters

Major Bernhard Jope, as he then was, shaking hands with Adolf Hitler on the occasion of the presentation of the Oak Leaves to the *Ritterkreuz*, at Berchtesgarden early in April 1944. Nearest the camera stands Major Kurt Bühligen, who flew Fw 190s with *JG 2* and ended the war credited with 112 victories, all in the west. Jope

might have sufficient fuel to return to the airfields from which they had taken off, the rest were to land at airfields on the Courland Peninsula in Latvia which was still in German hands.

Then the enthralled officers learned that *KG 30* was one of the two units earmarked to fly the 'Beethoven' combinations during Operation *Eisenhammer*.

'So that was why my pilots had re-trained to fly fighters. . . . We learned that many of the combinations earmarked for the operation were ready, and work on putting together the remainder was proceeding at

the highest priority. The first of these aircraft would be delivered to Ruzyne shortly and training for the operation was to begin immediately. We left that two-hour briefing breathless with excitement. The enemy had been having things his own way for too long; now, at last, we could see a chance for us to strike back hard.'

A few days after that initial briefing the first of the 'Beethoven' combinations arrived at Ruzyne.

'It looked such an ungainly machine, sitting at its dispersal point. This was a training version of 'Beethoven', on which the Ju 88 retained its normal crew cabin. There sat the pilot who was to land the thing at the end of the flight. The explosive head was fitted only for an operational flight, and when it was carried the combination could not be landed. To get into the cockpit of the fighter, one had to climb up a long ladder placed against the wing. Climbing it, I felt rather like a window cleaner! The cockpit of the fighter was about 5.5 m [18 ft] high, which felt a bit odd. But when I was seated my head was in fact little higher than when I was in a Focke Wulf Kondor on the ground.

'In the Fw 190 there was a small extra panel underneath the main instrument panel, which carried the instruments and switches to control the Ju 88. The main flying controls were controlled by the movement of those in the fighter. There were separate controls to raise the undercarriage of the bomber after take-off.'

During training flights the undercarriage of the Fw 190 remained locked down. The path of travel of the inward-folding legs was blocked by the struts supporting the fuselage of the fighter.

'The big day came when I made my first flight in the "Beethoven". Possibly because I expected all sorts of difficulties with this unusual aircraft, and therefore handled it even more carefully than was usual with a new type, my first flight was a bit of an anti-climax. I simply started up, taxied out, took off and tried a few turns to get the feel of the thing; it was all quite straightforward. So far as I can remember, none of my other pilots had any problems with the combination either. The initial flights were made with the lower component carrying little fuel and no

warhead, so it was not very heavy and this made the combination easy to handle. During later flights the lower component was made progressively heavier.'

Although the combination was easy enough to fly, Jope and other pilots noticed that the machine had an unusual feel about it.

'One was sitting in a fighter, but the controls had the feel of those of a bomber. It handled like a normal Junkers 88, but there was a little more inertia during manoeuvres and one had to be careful especially when close to the ground. In flight all three engines were kept running; on their power the combination was, perhaps surprisingly, about 50 k.m./h. [30 m.p.h.] faster then the equivalent version of the Ju 88 by itself. If there was an engine failure, the combination handled like any other three-engined aircraft. If the centre engine failed there was no problem, because one was left with an ordinary twin-engined aircraft. If one of the bomber's engines failed, there was less of a tendency to swing than with a normal twin-engined type. Engine handling was in many ways similar to that of the old *Tante Ju*, the Junkers 52 three-engined transport. I never lost an engine while flying the "Beethoven", but I anticipated no serious problems if it had occurred.'

On an operational sortie, the pilot would use manual control only during the initial and final parts of the flight. For the rest of the flight the combination was to run on automatic pilot.

'The pilot could select one of two positions: *Reiseflug* [cruising flight] or *Automatik*. The in-flight manoeuvres were made on *Reiseflug*; on this setting the

these marauders. 'On one occasion Spitfires carried out a low-level strafing attack on Ruzyne, shooting up some of our aircraft. Our flak defences opened up, but the British pilots demonstrated their contempt for the gunners' efforts by performing victory rolls as they climbed away. We were most impressed by this display by the sporting Royal Air Force.'

Early in the retraining programme, Jope received orders to hand over command of *KG 30* to Oberst Hans Heise. Heise had considerable experience of air operations on the Eastern Front, and was better qualified to lead the unit during Operation *Eisenhammer*.

'I moved out to take up a staff appointment, but in the event I did not miss anything. The war situation deteriorated so rapidly that by the time there were sufficient aircraft and trained crews to carry out the operation against the power stations, at the end of March 1945, the necessary forward airfields had been lost to the enemy. The targets were beyond the reach of "Beethoven", and Operation *Eisenhammer* had to be abandoned. Those combinations that were not destroyed on the ground, either by enemy or by our own troops as they withdrew, were expended against the Russian crossings over the Oder river.

'For my part, I never doubted that had the necessary airfields been available, the "Beethoven" attack on the Russian power stations would have caused considerable disruption to the enemy war economy. Whether this would have had any serious effect on the course of the war is a matter for debate but one thing is certain: had that attack been mounted, it would have made a wonderful story for this book!'

A view from the rear of a 'Beethoven' combination, showing the improvised boarding arrangements for the pilot.

movements of the stick and rudder pedals in the fighter were relayed electrically to the automatic pilot in the Ju 88. On *Automatik* the autopilot held the aircraft on whatever heading or altitude had been established; this position could be selected to ease the pilot's work load on the way to the target, and was also used when the combination was lined up on the target immediately before the pilot fired the explosive bolts to disengage the fighter.'

During their training flights in the 'Beethoven' the German pilots had to keep their eyes open for Allied long range fighters. In the rapidly contracting area still held by German forces, there was nowhere safe from

A photograph taken by an Allied reconnaissance aircraft of Prague/Ruzyne airfield on 20 February 1945. It depicts seven 'Beethoven' combinations of
Kampfgeschwader 30, Jope's unit, soon after training began. Although the fighters mounted above the Junkers 88s are barely visible, their shadows show up clearly.

Inside the cockpit of the Fw 190 half of the 'Beethoven' combination. The central panel carried the auto-pilot controls and the propeller pitch indicators and combined boost/r.p.m. gauges for the Ju 88's engines. This panel bears all the signs of having been hastily installed.

CHAPTER 22

NIGHT *JABO*

'In general, I believe that night attacks are good only when one is so weak that one dare not attack the enemy in daylight.'

Frederick the Great

Even today, night ground-attack operations are considered to be one of the most difficult aspects of combat flying. They require a high degree of skill and training, and meticulous planning. Fähnenjunker Feldwebel Franz Züger flew the Fw 190F in this role during the early months of 1945. From 1942 until the middle of 1944 he had served as a flying instructor, teaching pilots to fly the Dornier Do 17, the Heinkel He 111 and the Junkers Ju 52. In August 1944 he was posted to *Schnellkampfgeschwader 107* at Tutow near Rostock, a unit training pilots to fly the Fw 190 fighter-bomber. He was fortunate in having amassed a large number of flying hours earlier in the war, for the new unit had neither the time nor the fuel to provide comprehensive training in the new role.

'At Tutow the conversion course was rudimentary in the extreme. We were simply shown round the cockpit and given a set of pilots' notes. When we felt we were ready for our first flight we mentioned it to our "instructor", who gave us an aircraft and off we went. By that time I was quite an experienced pilot and I had little trouble getting the Focke Wulf airborne. I merely held the stick

central, pushed open the throttle and the next thing I knew I was airborne. Landing this lively aircraft was, however, another matter. The first time I tried it I had to abandon the first five or six approaches. Each time, feeling I was likely to undershoot the runway, I had applied what would have been sufficient power to extend the glide of a bomber. That was far too much for the Focke Wulf, and each time it would leap away like a whipped racehorse. In the end I learned to ease the throttle open by the required small amount and I put down the fighter safely. After a few more trips in the Fw 190 I began to feel at home with it and found it a pleasant and docile machine to fly.'

Once Züger was judged ready for operations, he was sent on a few ground-attack missions against Russian troops advancing into Poland. He also flew a few *Wilde Sau* night-fighter sorties over Berlin, attempting without success to engage RAF bombers.

Then, in January 1945, Züger was sent to *Ergänzungskampfstaffel (Nacht)*, a training unit at Staaken near Berlin where pilots were initiated into the mysteries of

Fw 190A-5 modified for night-fighter bomber operations. As well as landing lights in the port wing, it had flat plates mounted above the engine exhausts to shield the pilot's eyes from the glare of the flames. VFW-Fokker

night ground-attack operations in the Fw 190F-8. This time the training was thorough, and it needed to be.

'At the bombing ranges at Jüterbog, south of Berlin, we carried out first day then night training attacks on targets marked for us by *Flieger Verbindungs Offiziere* [ground liaison officers]. By the end of the course we were able to navigate ourselves at night to the target area at altitudes below 300 m [1,000 ft]. At a previously designated pull-up point we would start our climb to an attack altitude of around 2,400 m [8,000 ft], at the same time warning the ground liaison officer that we were coming. The aim was to be over the target at the correct altitude with our speed well down. We then called the ground liaison officer again, and he would mark the target with flares. Once the flares were in view we would head towards them; as they disappeared under the leading edge of the wing close to the engine we would count "1 – 2 – 3 – 4", then roll the aircraft upside down. By putting one's head right back against the armour one could see the illuminated target. Then one had to pull back on the stick until the target was in front of the Revi sight.

'During the dive, made at an angle of about 40 degrees, the propeller blades were set to fine pitch so that they acted as an airbrake to prevent speed building up too rapidly. As soon as the target was in the centre of the Revi one held it there for a few seconds, then eased back slightly on the stick so that the bomb would clear the propeller and pressed the release button. For safety reasons the minimum release altitude was around 1,000 m [3,300 ft] and by the time we got there our speed was around 615 k.m./h. [380 m.p.h.]; after the release we pulled out of the dive, then descended below 300 m for the return flight.'

When a novice pilot made this type of attack in pitch darkness it was all too easy to become disorientated, especially during the roll-over and pull-through before he was established in the dive. Considerable practice was necessary before a pilot was judged proficient. Each new step in the training process was tried out first in daylight, then at night. A night attack on the range with a 500 kg [1,100 lb] cement training bomb was the final exercise during the training course.

At the beginning of February 1945, like several other operational training units, *Ergänzungskampfstaffel (Nacht)* was thrown into action in the desperate attempts to stem the fast-moving Soviet advance into East Prussia.

'Operating by day from Staaken and Rangsdorf near Berlin, we carried out low-level attacks on targets in the areas around Zellin, Kalenszig and Klewitz. Russian tanks were streaming across the frozen Oder river. We attacked them with 250 kg [550 lb] bombs; the object was to score hits either on the tanks, or near misses that would split the ice and cause the tanks to fall through. On other occasions we made strafing attacks and released containers of SD-2 and SD-4 cluster bombs. During these operations the Russian fighters gave us little trouble, but the light flak was murderous. During our four days in action every one of our aircraft was hit and we lost four pilots out of twelve.'

A few days later, Züger was posted to Italy to join the newly formed 3. *Staffel* of *Nachtschlachtgruppe* 9. The other two *Staffeln* in the *Gruppe* operated the Junkers Ju 87 in the night ground-attack role.

Fähnenjunker Feldwebel Franz Züger flew night ground-attack missions in Italy. *Züger*

those on the bombing range at Jüterbog. For one thing the targets were usually far beyond the front line, so there was no ground liaison officer to do the marking for us. In practice this meant that to achieve any sort of bombing accuracy, we could attack only on clear moonlight nights. A further change was that instead of the half-roll and pull-through type of attack used during training, we used the simpler method of approaching to one side of the target. As it disappeared under the wing, we banked into the dive. That enabled us to keep the unmarked target in view almost the whole time, and our speed did not build up so rapidly when we entered the dive.'

During these night operations the Focke Wulfs flew solo. The missions required careful pre-flight planning, and the *Gruppe* staff included a specialist navigation officer to assist pilots. The airfield had its own radio beacon, which was a great help in providing homings during the return flights.

Once the fighter-bomber pilots had released their bombs and were on their return flights over enemy territory, they were ordered to make strafing attacks on any enemy road vehicles they saw: 'Sometimes the lorry drivers got a bit careless and drove with their lights on, which provided us with a bit of sport. But usually at night there was little to be seen over the other side of the lines. Nevertheless it was frowned upon if we came back with a full ammunition load. So we would fire a few bursts into the "enemy darkness", to keep everyone happy.'

Typical of the attacks made by Züger's unit were those against Bologna on the nights of 22, 23 and 24 April 1945, to support the German paratroops cut off in the city. For these missions the Focke Wulfs operated from Villa Franca.

'By the time I reached Italy, the front was beginning to fall to pieces and we were moved around quite a lot. Typical of the airfields we used was that at Villa Franca near Verona. By day our aircraft were dispersed in the surrounding fields, carefully camouflaged in small individual revetments made from piled stones. Looking after us we had a *Batterie* of light flak, with 37-mm and quadruple-barrelled 20-mm weapons. They were very good, and whenever enemy aircraft came near the field the gunners would give them a rough time.

'The attacks we made against Allied positions in Italy differed somewhat from

A few Fw 190s were fitted with the FuG 101 radio altimeter, which made it possible to fly safely at low altitude at night or in poor visibility. The downwards looking aerials, one for transmission and one for reception, used the underside of the port wing as a reflector. VFW-Fokker

'Since the target was only about 110 km [70 miles] from the airfield, less than twenty minutes flying, we did not bother with a low altitude approach. Instead we climbed straight ahead and flew an almost direct route to the target at altitudes around 4,000 m [13,000 ft], jinking from time to time in case there were night-fighters about. The nights were clear, and with a battle raging in the city we could see the burning buildings from some distance away. We were briefed to hit a group of buildings on the northern side, so the paratroops could get out. On each night we operated in full *Staffel* strength, making standard dive attacks with 550 kg

[1,100 lb] bombs; the buildings were flattened.

'On the way out and back we were fortunate to have assistance from *Freya* radar stations situated along the southern face of the Alps. As well as providing navigational help, these were invaluable in giving warnings of the presence of enemy night-fighters. Radio calls such as "*Kleine Eule von rechts*" (Little owl [enemy night-fighter] coming from the right) never went unheeded.'

During operations the attacking German pilots maintained strict radio discipline, using their sets only for essential calls. But whenever they used the R/T, they were likely to receive a 'commercial' from the other side.

'"*Kameraden der deutschen Luftwaffe, kommt zu uns . . .*" [comrades of the German air force, come over to us . . .] Then would follow detailed instructions of how to reach certain designated airfields in order to surrender. Once that lot started we could not get a word in edgeways on that frequency, so we had to change to a secondary. But within a minute of our making a call on the new frequency, up he would come again: "*Kameraden der deutschen Luftwaffe . . . .*" I must say, they were triers! But I never heard of any of our aircraft in Italy going over to the enemy.'

Once Allied night-fighters discovered where the Focke Wulfs were based, they would mount standing patrols which would wait to catch the German fighter-bombers. Then, getting back to the airfield after a mission became something of an adventure.

'So we had to use a little cunning. As each aircraft took off, the airfield lighting was switched off. Back over the airfield after a mission, we would flash our navigation lights to identify ourselves. My aircraft was number 8, so I had to flash my lights eight times. The people on the ground acknowledged by flashing the runway lights on eight times. During the cross-wind leg, before turning in to land, I flashed the navigation lights again, one long flash then two short ones. This too would be similarly acknowledged from the ground, and gave me a final check of the position of the airfield. Then I would lower the flaps and undercarriage. When established on the final approach for

landing, I flashed the aircraft's lights long – short – long. On that signal the runway lights came on and stayed on until I was down.

'As soon as the aircraft landed, the place was plunged into darkness once again. As I rolled to a stop at the end of the runway, a motor cycle pulled in front of the aircraft. Following the dim red lamp on the rear, I taxied back to our revetment. We lost very few aircraft to enemy night-fighters. But several were wrecked in landing accidents, usually the result of a pilot making a bad approach and coming in too fast.'

To make things as difficult as possible for the enemy night-fighters trying to strafe its airfield, Züger's unit made frequent changes to the landing procedure. Normally the flare path employed at Luftwaffe airfields comprised two green lamps marking the touchdown point, a line of six or seven white lamps down the right hand side of the runway, and two red lamps marking the end of the runway. Sometimes the unit had the lamps repositioned, so that the reds marked the touchdown point instead of the stopping point: or the white lamps might mark the left side of the runway instead of the right. On occasions this subterfuge was successful, and led Allied night-fighters to strafe a disused part of the landing ground.

At the end of April 1945, the German withdrawal from Italy degenerated into a rout. 'We made our final attack on 29 April from Thiene near Verona. Then we withdrew to Innsbruck in Austria, just before the ceasefire for German forces in the south was announced on 2 May. We destroyed our trusty Focke Wulfs, then disbanded our unit. There was nothing to do but go home, so I began the 730 km [450 mile] walk to Bremen where my wife was.'

CHAPTER 23

UNITS EQUIPPED WITH FW 190S 9 APRIL 1945[1]

LUFTFLOTTE 4

Unit	Total	Serviceable
Schlachtgeschwader 2		
I. Gruppe	33	21
Schlachtgeschwader 10		
Stab	6	4
I. Gruppe	23	21
II. Gruppe	24	15
III. Gruppe	30	17

LUFTFLOTTE 6

Unit	Total	Serviceable
Jagdgeschwader 3		
Stab	4	4
IV. Gruppe	61	56
Jagdgeschwader 6		
Stab	4	4[2]
I. Gruppe	72	59
II. Gruppe	48	45
Jagdgeschwader 11		
Stab	4	4
I. Gruppe	55	53
III. Gruppe	54	51

Unit	Total	Serviceable
Schlachtgeschwader 1		
Stab	3	2
I. Gruppe	40	39
II. Gruppe	44	38
III. Gruppe	42	36
Schlachtgeschwader 2		
Stab	6	6
II. Gruppe	44	38
Schlachtgeschwader 3		
Stab	8	4
II. Gruppe	47	43
Schlachtgeschwader 4		
I. Gruppe	30	24
II. Gruppe	39	39
III. Gruppe	24	20
Schlachtgeschwader 9		
I. Gruppe	59	54
Schlachtgeschwader 77		
Stab	8	8
I. Gruppe	34	34
II. Gruppe	34	27
III. Gruppe	47	46
Schlachtgeschwader 151		
13. Staffel	18	17
Nahaufklärungsgruppe 31	15	12[3]

LUFTFLOTTE (REICH)

Unit	Total	Serviceable
Jagdgeschwader 2		
I. Gruppe	5	3
II. Gruppe	8	4
III. Gruppe	12	9
Jagdgeschwader 4		
Stab	6	4
II. Gruppe	50	34

The final production version of the Fw 190 family was the Tank 152H, a major redesign of the fighter with a lengthened wing for high altitude operations. Powered by a liquid-cooled Junkers Jumo 213 in-line engine, the fighter had a maximum speed of 472 m.p.h. at 41,000 ft (760 k.m./h at 1,2500 m). That performance was close to the limits of what was possible using a piston engine. VFW-Fokker

Two more views of the Tank 152H.

Just before the end of the war a few Tank 152Hs went into action with *Jagdgeschwader 301*. Taken in March or April 1945, this photograph shows aircraft of *Stab* and *III. Gruppe* at readiness at Alteno bei Luckau, south of Berlin.

Unit	Total	Serviceable
Jagdgeschwader 26		
Stab	4	3
I. Gruppe	44	16
II. Gruppe	57	29
III. Gruppe	35	15
Jagdgeschwader 301		
Stab (operating the Ta 152)	3	2
I. Gruppe	35	24
II. Gruppe	32	15
Jagdgruppe 10	15	9
Nachtschlachtgruppe 20	27	11
Kampfgeschwader 200		
III. Gruppe	31	21[4]

LUFTFLOTTENKOMMANDO (EAST PRUSSIA)

Unit	Total	Serviceable
Jagdgeschwader 51		
Stab	20	11

Unit	Total	Serviceable
Schlachtgeschwader 3		
I. Gruppe	27	24

Luftwaffe General (Norway)

Unit	Total	Serviceable
Jagdgeschwader 5		
IV. Gruppe	about 20	about 15[5]
Aufklärungsgruppe 32	about 10	about 5[5]

Luftwaffenkommando (Courland)

Unit	Total	Serviceable
Jagdgeschwader 54		
Stab	5	5
I. Gruppe	38	33
II. Gruppe	41	38
Schlachtgeschwader 3		
III. Gruppe	43	41
Nahaufklärungsgruppe 5	25	18[5]

Luftwaffe General (Italy)

Unit	Total	Serviceable
Nachtschlachtgruppe 9	38	35[6]
Nahaufklärungsgruppe 11	24	14[5]

Notes

1. By this stage of the war Luftflotten 4, 6 and Reich, the only three major fighting formations remaining in existence, had been squeezed back into Germany itself or the small neighbouring territories still under German occupation. In the final chaos of near-defeat they no longer confined their operations to defined geographical areas, and because of that their combat zones are not stated in the table above.
2. Unit also operated Bf 109s.
3. Unit also operated the Siebel Si 204.
4. Fighter-bomber unit.
5. In the mounting chaos the strength returns for Luftwaffe General Norway were not included in the official record. The figures given here are approximate.
6. Unit also operated Ju 87s.

CHAPTER 24

FINALE

The following excerpts were taken from the flying logbook of Leutnant Helmut Wenk, who flew Fw 190F-9 fighter-bombers with the *III./Schlachtgeschwader I*. They convey a vivid impression of the hectic actions fought during the losing battle north of Berlin in the final week of the war. During that seven day period, the unit was forced to move its base four times.

Date	Time: From To	Route	Enemy Activity	Results of Flight
27.4	1440 540	Neubrandenburg – west of Prenzlau – Gollmitz – Neubrandenburg	Light flak, fighters	1 × 250 kg container with SD-4 hollow-charge bombs released in the dive from 1,500 m [4,800 ft], on the road through the wood near Gollmitz. Precise result not observed, but the bombs fell in the target area. Attacked a self-propelled gun from low altitude, results not observed. Air combat with four La 5s; one fired at, disappeared into a layer of cloud.
27.4	1850 1945	Neubrandenburg – west of Prenzlau – near Boizen – Neubrandenburg	Light and medium flak, fighters	1 × 250 kg container and 4 × 50 kg bombs released in the dive from 2,275 m [7,400 ft], on the briefed target at the corner of the wood near Zervelin. Due to poor light, results not observed. Ten La 5s tried to intercept and fired at the second Rotte.
28.4	1635	Neubrandenburg – east of Neubrandenburg – Neubrandenburg	Light flak	Reconnaissance flight at between 1,000 m [3,300 ft] and ground level. Enemy armour and troops to the east and south-east of Neubrandenburg, seen to advancing. Bad weather and rain showers, cloud base in places 200 m [700 ft]. After this report an operation was flown against this target, then the unit withdrew to Barth.

An Fw 190A-8 seen carrying the experimental Blohm und Voss Bv 246 *Hagelkorn* (hailstone) unpowered glider bomb, at Karlshagen in the summer of 1944. The testing of this weapon continued until the end of the war with various types of guidance, but it was never used operationally. via Selinger

Date	Time: From To	Route	Enemy Activity	Results of Flight
28.4	1805 1900	Neubrandenburg – east of town of Burgstargard – Barth	Light flak	1 × 500 kg armour-piercing bomb from 400 m [1,300 ft] on the road through the wood on the outskirts of Burgstargard. Target hit.
29.4	1540 1625	Barth – Treptow – Barth	Light flak, fighters	1 × 500 kg armour-piercing bomb on the road where columns passing, east of Treptow. Low altitude attack, hit observed. Air combat with Yak 3, no results observed.
29.4	1800 1850	Barth – Treptow – Barth	Light flak	1 × 250 kg container and 4 × 50 kg bombs released on the column at the previous target. Due to thick smoke, results not observed. Oblt Lehn [his wing man] crashed on take-off and killed.
30.4	1030 1140	Barth – Neubrandenburg – Barth	Nil	*Schwarm* leader became disorientated in cloud, ran short of fuel. 1 × 500 kg bomb jettisoned.
30.4	1700 1745	Barth – east of Greifswald – Barth	Nil	The roads in the target area were found to be again in our hands and the roads in the enemy occupied area were all packed with refugees. 1 × 500 kg bomb jettisoned.
30.4	1930 2015	Barth – east of Greifswald – Wismar	Light flak	1 × 500 kg and 4 × 50 kg bombs on a column of enemy vehicles heading for the outskirts of the town. Bombs laid accurately. Tanker vehicle hit, thick smoke seen clearly.
2.5	1400 1500	Wismar – Barth – Flensburg	Fighters (Thunder bolts). Hit twice by own flak	Russians and English almost at airfield. Transfer to Flensburg.

Cease fire on 3.5.45 at 0800 hours, on the orders of Grossadmiral Doenitz.

FOLLOWING A PARADE WITH A SOLEMN ADDRESS BY THE COMMANDER AND THE SINGING OF THE NATIONAL ANTHEM, *SCHLACHTGESCHWADER I* WITH A TOTAL STRENGTH OF ONE *GRUPPE* OF ABOUT 30 AIRCRAFT, UNDEFEATED BY THE ENEMY, DISBANDED ITSELF INTO SMALL GROUPS TO MAKE THEIR WAY HOME, PLEDGED TO CONTINUE TO DO THEIR DUTY AND BUILD A NEW, BETTER, GERMANY.

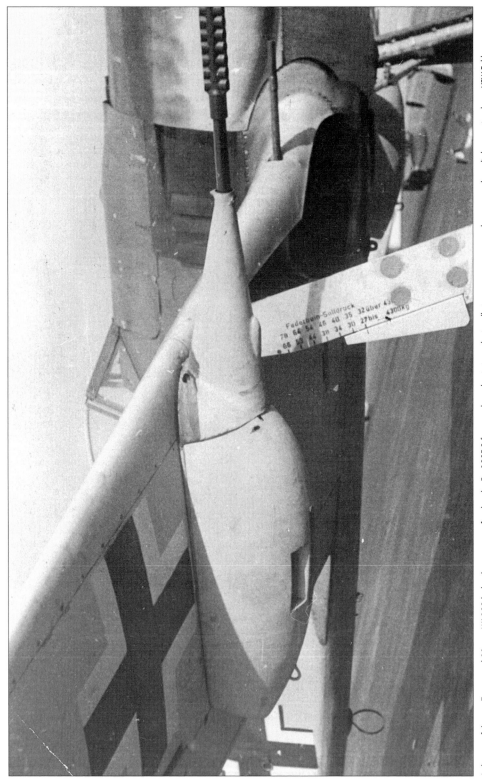

A close up of the nacelle mounted 30-mm MK 103 high velocity cannon, fitted to the Fw 190F-8 for ground-attack missions; the installation was not a success, however, and saw little operational use. VFW-Fokker

CHAPTER 25

FW 190s Post War

After the war a few Fw 190A-8s served with the French Air Force under the designation NC 900.

Fw 190Ds flown by the trials unit of the Red Air Force after the war.

Strange bedfellows: a pair of Fw 190s in formation with a Spitfire V of the Turkish Air Force. They received both types during the war and continued to fly them for some years after it.

APPENDIX A

PRODUCTION OF FW 190 AND TA 152

Year	Quantity
1941	1,224
1942	1,878
1943	3,208
1944	11,401
1945 (to first week in May)	approx. 2,700
1945 production of Ta 152	approx. 160
Grand Total (all versions)	approx. 19,570

APPENDIX B

FW 190 UNIT PREFIXES

Fw 190 *Geschwader* and *Gruppen* carried the following prefixes to denote the operational roles in which they were employed:

Aufklärungs-	Reconnaissance
Erprobungs-	Test
Fernaufklärungs-	Long Range Reconnaissance
Jagd-	Fighter
Jagdbomber-	Fighter-Bomber
Kampf-	Bomber
Nachtjagd-	Night-Fighter
Nachtschlacht-	Night Ground-Attack
Nahaufklärungs-	Short Range Reconnaissance
Schnellkampf-	High Speed Bomber
Sturm-	Operated Fw 190 fighters fitted with extra armour, to carry out attacks on US heavy bombers from close range.

APPENDIX C

LUFTWAFFE FLYING UNITS

THE STAFFEL

During the early part of the war the *Staffel* (plural *Staffeln*) had a nominal strength of nine aircraft, and it was the smallest combat flying unit in general use in the Luftwaffe. During the final year of the war many fighter *Staffeln* had their establishment increased to sixteen aircraft.

THE GRUPPE

The *Gruppe* (plural *Gruppen*) was the basic flying unit of the Luftwaffe for operational and administrative purposes. Initially it was established at three *Staffeln* each with nine aircraft, plus a *Stab* Flight with three, making thirty aircraft in all. The *Staffeln* were designated using Arabic numbers. Thus the 1st, 2nd and 3rd *Staffeln* belonged to the Ist *Gruppe*, the 4th, 5th and 6th belonged to the IInd *Gruppe*, the 7th, 8th and 9th *Staffeln* belonged to the IIIrd *Gruppe*.

During the mid-war period each fighter *Gruppe* was strengthened by the addition of a fourth *Staffel*. With the increase to the sixteen aircraft establishment for a *Staffel*, this brought some *Gruppen* to a strength of sixty-seven aircraft.

THE GESCHWADER

The *Geschwader* (plural *Geschwader*) was the largest flying unit in the Luftwaffe to have a fixed nominal strength, initially three *Gruppen* with a total of ninety aircraft, and a *Stab* unit of four, making a total of ninety-four aircraft.

In the mid-war period each fighter *Geschwader* was strengthened by the addition of a IVth *Gruppe*. Where this was the case, and each *Gruppe* comprised four *Staffeln*, the numbering of the latter within the *Gruppen* was changed. Now the 1st, 2nd, 3rd and 4th *Staffeln* belonged to the Ist *Gruppe*, the 5th, 6th, 7th and 8th *Staffeln* belonged to the IInd *Gruppe*, the 9th, 10th, 11th and 12th *Staffeln* belonged to the IIIrd *Gruppe*, and the 13th, 14th, 15th and 16th *Staffeln* belonged to the IVth *Gruppe*

THE FLIEGERKORPS (AIR CORPS) AND LUFTFLOTTE (AIR FLEET)

The Air Corps and the larger Air Fleet varied in size and each comprised a balanced force of all types of combat aircraft. The number of *Gruppen* assigned to these formations depended on the importance of their assigned operational area.

APPENDIX D

EQUIVALENT WARTIME RANKS

Luftwaffe	Royal Air Force	USAAF
Generalfeldmarschal	Marshal of the R.A.F	(no equivalent)
Generaloberst	Air Chief Marshal	General (4 star)
General der Flieger	Air Marshal	General (3 star)
Generalleutnant	Air Vice-Marshal	General (2 star)
Generalmajor	Air Commodore	General (1 star)
Oberst	Group Captain	Colonel
Oberstleutnant	Wing Commander	Lieutenant Colonel
Major	Squadron Leader	Major
Hauptmann	Flight Lieutenant	Captain
Oberleutnant	Flying Officer	1st Lieutenant
Leutnant	Pilot Officer	2nd Lieutenant
Stabsfeldwebel	Warrant Officer	Warrant Officer
Oberfeldwebel	Flight Sergeant	Master Sergeant
Feldwebel	Sergeant	Technical Sergeant
Unterfeldwebel	(no equivalent)	(no equivalent)
Unteroffizier	Corporal	Staff Sergeant
Hauptgefreiter	(no equivalent)	Sergeant
Obergefreiter	Leading Aircraftman	Corporal
Gefreiter	Aircraftman First Class	Private First Class
Flieger	Aircraftman Second Class	Private Second Class

INDEX

Adolph, Hauptmann Walter 25
Aircraft types, Allied
    B-17 Flying Fortress 59–66, 70
    P-38 Lightning 52–3, 115–16, 119
    P-51 Mustang 9, 51–2, 105–6, 149
    Spitfire V 47–9
    Spitfire IX 28, 49–51
    Spitfire with Griffon engine 54
    Spitfire XIV 39, 106–7
    Typhoon 53–4
Aircraft types, German
    Dornier Do 217 162
    Junkers Ju 88 162–7
    Messerschmitt Bf 109 1, 75, 123

'Beethoven' device 162–70
Blumer, Captain Lawrence, USAAF 119
Bonin, Hauptmann Hubertus von 62
Buchholz, Feldwebel Fritz 113–18

Canterbury, attack on 75–7
Captured Fw 190, examination by RAF 39–55

Deer, Squadron Leader Alan 28
Dilg, Feldwebel Adolf 75–82, 148–52
Douglas, Air Chief Marshal Sir Sholto ix, 38, 39

Eisenhammer, Operation 162–70
ejector seat 14, 15, 17, 20

Fighter control bunker 71
Focke Wulf Fw 190
    Armament
        Additional cannon fitted 69
        Blohm und Voss Bv 246 missile 183
        Wgr 21 rocket 72–4
        Installation of SG 113 weapon 146

        Rheinmetall-Borsig MK 108 cannon 128
        Test of X-4 missile 138–9
    British plan to hijack 31–7
    Design concept 1–4
    Fighter-bomber role 75–82, 87–95, 170–5
    Fitted with BMW 801 engine 8
    Front line units
        27 July 1942 56–8
        17 May 1943 83–6
        31 May 1944 109–12
        9 April 1945 176–81
    Initial flight testing 10–24
    New variants
        Fw 190D 156–61
        Tank Ta 152 9, 178–80
        Two seat trainer 154, 155
    Night-fighter role 96–101
    Reconnaissance role 110, 112

Gail, Leutnant Werner 140–5
Glunz, Oberleutnant Adolf 67
Göring, Reichsmarschall Hermann 13, 97
Greisert, Hauptmann Heino 29

Hackfeld, Hauptmann Wilhelm 77, 78
Hackle, Major Anton 59, 63, 65
Hagenah, Leutnant Walther 120–7
Herrmann, Major Hajo 97

Jeschonnek, Generaloberst Hans 8
Jope, Oberst Bernard viii, 162–70

Luftwaffe units:
    Geschwader
        JG 1 61
        JG 2 28, 75, 78
        JG 11 59

JG 26 25, 28, 59, 75
JG 51 102–4
JG 54 62
JG 301 180
KG 30 162–70
Nachtjagdgeschwader 10 98
Schnellkampfgeschwader 10 78, 84, 87–95
Gruppen
   IV./(Sturm) JG 3 120–7
   II./(Sturm) JG 4 127
   II./JG 6 113–18
   III./SG 3 140–5
   III./ZG 2 75
   II./(Sturm) JG 300 130–7

Mattscheibe tactic 97
Mayer, Major Egon 61, 62
Moritz, Hauptmann Wilhelm 125

Neptun radar 98–101
Nowotny, Hauptmann Walter 153

Papenburg, Obergefreiter Heinz 127
Pinckney, Captain Philip 31–7

Quill, Jeffrey 31, 37

Richthofen, Generalfeldmarschall Wolfram von 94
Royal Aircraft Establishment, Farnborough 38, 39
Royal Air Force Intelligence reports 25, 28

Sabotage, cases of 149
Sander, Hans 10–24
Schäfer, Feldwebel Hans 126
Schneider, Oberleutnant Walter 25
Schöpfel, Gerhard 29
Schröder, Unteroffizier Ernst 130–7
Stammberger, Oberleutnant Otto 59
Sturmgruppe, tactic 120–37

Tank, Kurt viii, 1–9, 24
Tutow, Fw 190 production facility 153

Udet, Generaloberst Ernst 8, 13

Wenk, Leutnant Helmut 87–90, 182, 184
Wilde Sau tactic 97
Wurmheller, Major Josef 66

Züger, Fähnenjunker Feldwebel Franz 170–5

Visit our website and discover thousands of other History Press books.
www.thehistorypress.co.uk